THE POOH PARTY BOOK

THE POOH PARTY BOOK

inspired by *Winnie-the-Pooh* and
The House at Pooh Corner

by A. A. MILNE

VIRGINIA H. ELLISON

illustrated by Ernest H. Shepard

E. P. DUTTON & CO., INC. NEW YORK

Also by Virginia H. Ellison

THE POOH COOK BOOK

Grateful acknowledgment is made to David McKay Co., Inc., for permission
to include the recipe for Violet Syrup from *Stalking the Healthful Herbs*
(1966) by Euell Gibbons.

Published simultaneously in Canada by McClelland and Stewart, Limited

SBN: 0-525-37480-9   LCC: 72-157943

Printed in the U.S.A.   First Edition

For Mother and Jan

and thanks to
Dave, Nick, and Vivian

Acknowledgments

Nick and Lisette Schaefer and their daughter, Lisette, by an oversight, were not thanked for providing me with pounds and pounds of their own delicious wild-flower honey for *The Pooh Cook Book* nor for the many delightful hours I spent with them, learning about beekeeping, honey extracting, and the uses of beeswax and honey. They did me the same service for the recipes in this book. I thank them now, in full measure.

I want also to thank friends and neighbors, near and far, but these twenty-two in particular: Barbara Falk and Heidi; Nancy Buckley, Lisa and Lynda; Akeita Somersille and her granddaughters, Claire, Carol, Susan, and Stephanie; Barbara Delafield, Dana and Beau; Barbara Baker and Joan Santandrea; and the six mothers in Savanna, Illinois, whom I do not know but who gladly tested recipes when asked by Gretchen Law—Vera Dorak, Almeta Cottral, Bernelle Weiler, Berenice Hussey, Mabelle Grieson, and Margaret Brennan. All these friends measured, diced, stirred, blended, boiled, baked, and frosted; some of them, in addition, cut, pasted, dyed, sewed, painted, and modeled. Their suggestions were many and made this book easier to work with and more imaginative than it would otherwise have been.

Gretchen Law, talented at sewing and cooking, has my deepest gratitude for her imaginative testing and suggestions, which were many.

Barbara Falk was responsible for a fruitful conversation with Harriet Smith, a Pooh enthusiast and handy with her needle.

Ethel Ramond gave me the recipe which became the Black Cloud Honey Cake with Walnut Bees, for which I thank her.

I am grateful to Mrs. Winifred Nazarian, who sent me a copy of an invitation she made for a Pooh breakfast which she gave for her four nieces. That invitation gave me ideas for those in this book.

I am in debt to Majorie Henderson for typing the manuscript and for giving me extra time when I needed to check details.

Finally, special thanks and love go to my family: Mabel and Dick Soskin, Sarah and Louis Chypre, Chard and Nicole; Jane and John Smithers; Kathy, Marty, and Dave Howell; to my almost family—Russ and Florence, Susan and Peter, Mark and Matthew Meyer; Gretchen and Si Law, Heather, Doug, and Rusty; Nan Law; Lillian and Bob Phillips; Alan and Stefan Sorvall; and to my friends— Beryl Barrow, Cornelia Ernst Zagat and her family, Caddy and Tim Eland, Nina and Tim Zagat, Janet Van Duyn, Pat and Mitch Reis, Mary and Charles Ramond, Alex Brooks, Ursula Gerhart, Evelyn Liotard, Elaine Minick, Gloria DuBissette, Marjorie and John Henville-Shannon, Marian and Bob Couturier, Felicity and Savin Hoffecker, Elizabeth Apperly, Jeanne Vance Davis, Yvonne Fuertes, Rosalind Rosenthal, Hilda Renfroe, Lee Schaefer Lucas, Billie Weil, Paul Kresch, Pen Schofield, Bob de Vries, Helen Mather, Bea Gilbert, Linda and Paul Draper, Louise and Paul Liebold, and to those dozens and dozens of other friends and acquaintances, old and new, who made the creation of this book all pleasure.

Contents

II. A SPRING PARTY

III. A PICNIC, SWIMMING, AND EXPOTITION PARTY

IV. A HONEY–TASTING PARTY FOR POOH

V. A WOOZLE–WIZZLE SNOW PARTY

Introduction

This book is about five different Pooh parties. They grew out of parties, or Very Nearly parties, in *Winnie-the-Pooh* and *The House at Pooh Corner,* and *they* grew out of things that were happening, or had happened, to Pooh or one of his friends.

Your parties will probably grow out of other things too—such as wanting to celebrate a birthday or a holiday; learning to swim; making a new friend or welcoming home an old one from a vacation; reading about Pooh and Piglet, Eeyore, Owl, Rabbit, and the others, for the first time or the tenth; or, as Christopher Robin put it, you might give a party "because of what someone did" that was helpful or kind or brave.

These are not the sitting-around kind of parties, although there are suggestions for quiet games and for cutting and pasting and coloring, and time enough for eating. This means that you can wear your next-best clothes, or even your next-best after those, so that you don't have to care whether you get a little dirt, rubber cement, paint, chocolate, or honey on them.

These are parties where everybody is invited to make things and be helped—or not, as the case may be—and everybody gets or makes a favor and at least one present. At these parties everybody can play games and get a prize for doing something, even if it's only for making the funniest Poster or Coloring Book; for playing a Pooh Musical Instrument; for being "It" the most times or the fewest. You can always invent a reason for giving a prize, so that no one goes home without one.

Allow plenty of time for getting ready for your party. That way it's more fun. And the more you practice making things, the easier they are to do. When you read the Invitations section, remember that your invitations should be ready to be mailed at least two weeks before the party. When you read the Decorations section, keep in mind that it might take as long as three weeks if you work for an hour or so a day, to decorate your tablecloth, paper napkins, plates, cups, and place cards.

Start collecting the equipment and materials you will need for the Things to Make and Games to Play section a good month in advance. Some of them you can save up or have friends or neighbors save, too; others you can borrow, so that you have enough of everything for the number of friends you expect at your party.

All the recipes for Things to Eat and Drink (which, of course, use lots of honey) and the directions for Things to Make and Games to Play have been tried and tested many times. But if a cake and a batch of cookies come out a little lopsided, it doesn't matter: they will still taste good, especially since you baked them. Or, if it's something you make, such as a basket, and it isn't perfect, it will still be useful for putting things in or for taking on a picnic. A Music Stand with drawings of Pooh that look more like Piglet, for example, can start everybody off making funny drawings of all the Pooh characters and might lead to creating funny Paper Bag Masks.

There are many ways to use this book. The first is to give each party just as it's described, in the course of a year or more. The second is to read straight through all the parties and pick out the one that's most appropriate for what you want to celebrate and for the time of year. A third is to give a Pooh party by choosing from each party those Things to Eat and Drink and Things to Make and Games to Play that you like best. The chances are that your friends will, too.

And the other way to use this book is to give a Pooh party because you *feel* like giving one—just for yourself. The feeling might come over you as you're brushing snow away from the front of your house, or on a fine spring morning when the sun has come back over the Forest, bringing with it the scent of May, or on some golden evening as you're walking home, and you *know* that you must do Something Special. When that feeling comes over you, it's time to go home and invite your friends. It's time to shout joyfully and think to yourself, as Pooh did, "A party for me? How grand!"

Virginia H. Ellison

Stamford, Connecticut
May, 1971

I

AN EEYORE
BIRTHDAY PARTY

"It's my birthday. The happiest day of the year."
Winnie-the-Pooh

Well, it just happened that you had been to a party the day before at the house of your friend Piglet, and you had balloons at the party.

Winnie-the-Pooh

Invitations

You might give an Eeyore Birthday Party for your best friend or to celebrate your own birthday.

The invitations should be made of red construction paper.

Fold them, so that they have a fold in the middle and fit mailing envelopes which can be bought in various sizes by the package.

Draw a good-sized balloon on the outside of the invitation. Write inside the balloon:

> Come give Many Happy Returns of the Day
> to
> *(name of friend)*

If the party is for you, write:

> Please come help celebrate my birthday
> Day: Date:
> Time: from   o'clock to   o'clock
>
>   *(your name)*
>   *(address)*
>   *(telephone number)*

On the inside of the invitation, write:

> This is a real birthday party for *(name of friend)* .
> Please bring a red balloon as a present, if you can.
> I have a Very Useful Pot to put the balloons in.

Decorations

TABLECLOTH AND NAPKINS,
PAPER PLATES AND CUPS

Cut balloon shapes from red construction paper. Glue them in bunches or in a scattered pattern on a white or pastel-colored paper tablecloth. Draw the strings, singly or in bunches, from the balloons with a black felt-tipped pen.

Around the edge of the tablecloth paste cutouts of Eeyore made from tracings on tan or gray construction paper. To make these, put tracing paper over the drawing of Eeyore on page 144 of this book, and, in soft pencil, follow the outline showing through. Put the tracing, tracing-side down, on the construction paper. Go back and forth on the back of the tracing paper with the soft pencil over the outline tracing. Remove the tracing paper and you have an outline of Eeyore to cut out. Or make freehand drawings of Eeyore on construction paper and cut them out.

While all this was happening, Piglet had gone back to his own house to get Eeyore's balloon.

Winnie-the-Pooh

CENTERPIECE

Red balloons and a honey pot made from a basket or a carton; or, best of all, use a big crock.

Put the name of a friend who will be at the party on each balloon. Use a felt-tipped pen, paint, or crayon.

If you like, draw Eeyore in a different pose on each balloon. See Chapter VI of *Winnie-the-Pooh*.

Blow up the balloons. Tie them with strings so the air can't escape.

Tie the free end of each string around a stone or a stick. Or weave them together and weight them down with anything heavy enough to hold them inside the honey pot.

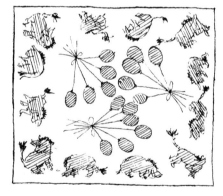

Things to Eat and Drink

HONEY NUT BREAD SANDWICHES

HONEY NUT BREAD

(Preheat oven to 350° F.)   *(Yield: 1 loaf)*

1 egg
¾ cup churned *or* creamed honey
1 cup sour milk *or* light cream

2 cups flour
1 teaspoon baking soda
½ teaspoon baking powder
1 cup nuts, in pieces
salt, if nuts are unsalted

Beat the egg and add the honey in a large bowl until well mixed.

Add the sour milk or cream and the dry ingredients (except the nuts), alternately, to the egg-honey mixture, stirring each time until well blended.

Add the nuts and stir again.

Bake for 1 hour or until a knife in the middle comes out dry and clean.

Remove from the baking pan after 10 minutes and let it cool on a rack.

SANDWICHES

This is delicious used in sandwiches made of cream cheese or peanut butter with or without a little currant, apple, or strawberry jelly spread on top.

EEYORE'S BIRTHDAY CAKE
WITH PINK ICING

CAKE

(Preheat oven to 350° F.)

1½ cups confectioners' sugar, sifted	1 Tablespoon honey
10 egg whites	1 teaspoon cream of tartar
8 egg yolks	1 cup cake flour
	tube pan

Do not butter the tube pan.

Beat the egg whites, gradually adding half the sugar after the eggs foam and begin to whiten.

Beat the egg yolks until thick and lemony. Add the honey and the cream of tartar.

Add the flour to the rest of the sugar, and this mixture to the egg yolks. Beat until well blended.

Fold in the egg whites. Do not beat.

Bake 45 to 50 minutes or until the cake springs back to the touch.

PINK ICING

1 egg white	red vegetable food coloring
1½ cups confectioners' sugar	
½ teaspoon honey	

Beat the egg white until stiff and gradually add the sugar and honey.

Add the red food coloring, a drop or two at a time to get the pink color you want.

Ice the cake when it is cool. Decorate it with three pink candles.

PINK HONEY LEMONADE

1 cup cranberry juice	strawberries *or*
1 quart lemonade, fresh *or* frozen	raspberries
	honey
	sprigs of mint

Add the cranberry juice to the lemonade in the amounts given.

Add a strawberry or two or a teaspoon of raspberries and ¼ teaspoon of honey to each glass before serving.

If you use fresh lemonade, sweeten with honey or sugar to taste.

Decorate with a sprig of mint.

"Thank you," said Eeyore. "Unexpected and gratifying, if a little lacking in Smack."

The House at Pooh Corner

THISTLE SNOW ICE CREAM SODA

1 teaspoon warm honey
 lavender *or* purple food
 coloring
½ cup milk

½ scoop vanilla ice cream
 fresh-fallen snow *or*
 crushed ice-cube snow

Mix the honey and the lavender food coloring together in
 a tall glass.
Add the milk and ice cream.
Stir until blended.
Fill the glass with snow.

Good for cooling off after party games.

"Of course, I've still got all this
snow to do what I like with. One
mustn't complain."

The House at Pooh Corner

Things to Make and Games to Play

Read through all the directions for Things to Make and Games to Play for An Eeyore Birthday Party. If you're having a small party with just a few friends, then you may want to make only Pooh Musical Instruments and Coloring Books or Eeyore Posters. If you're having a large party, then you will want your friends to take turns making different things. Get together all the materials you will need, so that you have everything ready for your friends when they come to the party.

Not everyone need make one each of the things suggested. Some might; some might not. While some friends are making Posters or Coloring Books, others might make Book and Music Stands, and the rest, Musical Instruments.

If you're going to play Pin the Tail on Eeyore and you're making your own game, make an Eeyore's Lost-Tail Bookmark for each friend who will be at the party. *And* one for yourself.

PICKING THISTLES

For all games where you have to choose somebody to be "It" or somebody to start first, try "picking thistles."

Use white cardboard. Color it lavender. Or use lavender-colored drinking straws.

Cut cardboard or straws of different lengths, one for each friend. The cardboard straws should be a little wider than your thumb.

Hold the thistles in your closed fist, so that they are all even at the top and no one can see which are longer or shorter. Use your other fist, if necessary, to hide the bottoms of the straws. Or put them on a table so that they are even at one end. Cover the uneven ends with a book.

Each friend picks a thistle. The one who get the shortest gets first choice of the Things to Make. The one who picks the next shortest gets the next choice, and so on. Whoever picks the longest straw will have last choice.

EEYORE POSTERS

large pieces of wrapping paper *or* brown paper bags
cardboard, wood, plasterboard, *or* fiberboard
staples, needle and thread, glue, *or* thumbtacks
copies of *Winnie-the-Pooh* and *The House at Pooh Corner*
paints, felt-tipped pens, colored pencils, *or* crayons
pushpins *or* tape

Before the party, make up two or three big pads of poster paper. They can be made of wrapping paper or big paper bags which have been cut, made even top and bottom, ironed flat, and stapled, sewn, glued, or tacked together on a piece of cardboard, wood, plasterboard, fiberboard, or other backing material.

Have copies of *Winnie-the-Pooh, The House at Pooh Corner,* and this book, so that two friends can share a book, or ask each friend to bring his copy of either of these Pooh books.

Let each two friends sharing a book choose the picture or pictures they want as the inspiration for their posters.

The posters need not be copies of the Pooh drawings. Let

each friend choose the colors and the kinds of paints, felt-tipped pens, colored pencils, or crayons he wants to use.

Some friends might like to make very naturalistic posters; others, imaginative and abstract pictures of Pooh characters and scenes. Let the friends put their names in small letters on the posters. Use the posters to decorate the party room walls.

If it's an outdoor party, perhaps you could use pushpins or tape the posters to a wall, a tree, or a fence. Let friends who want to, take home their posters to hang in their rooms.

"I gave him a box of paints to paint things with."

Winnie-the-Pooh

POOH PENCIL PUPPETS

pipe cleaners in different colors
crayons, felt-tipped pens, *or* paints
glue *or* rubber cement
wool *or* heavy cotton thread
   for hair *or* whiskers

pencils with
   erasers
paper
scissors
thumbtacks

Bend the pipe cleaners in the skeletal shapes of the Pooh characters.

Cut body shapes, arms, legs, ears, and faces out of paper for each character that you make. For Christopher Robin make a face and clothes.

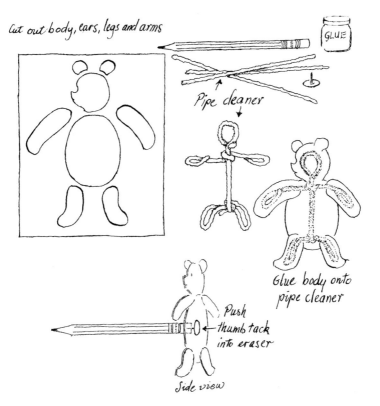

Cut out body, ears, legs and arms

GLUE

Pipe cleaner

Glue body onto
pipe cleaner

Push
thumb tack
into eraser

Side view

Color on eyes, noses, and mouths with crayons, felt-tipped pens, or paints.

Glue the cutout bodies, arms, legs, and last of all, the hair, or whiskers, onto the pipe cleaners.

Push a thumbtack under a pipe cleaner in the center or above the center of the puppet and into the eraser of a pencil, so that the pencil is at a right angle to the body of the puppet.

Now you're ready to put on a Pooh Puppet Show, using one friend as narrator or reader and the others as characters from a favorite chapter of *Winnie-the-Pooh* or *The House at Pooh Corner*.

Use the party table or a big carton, with Pooh decorations, on a table as the stage.

"*That* was what I wanted to ask you," said Pooh. "Because my spelling is Wobbly. It's good spelling but it Wobbles, and the letters get in the wrong places."

Winnie-the-Pooh

natural-colored cloth with visible weave,
    8½″ × 4¾″
big-eyed needle for wool
embroidery wool, gray and black
light cardboard, 8″ × 2″

Be sure to choose a piece of cloth where you can easily see the weave, so that the stitchery of Eeyore on the front of the bookmark will be easy.

Measure in 1½ inches from one edge and 1¼ inches from the other edge, and very lightly draw lines down the cloth from top to bottom.

Between the lines, and a little above the middle, trace or draw an outline picture of Eeyore without his tail.

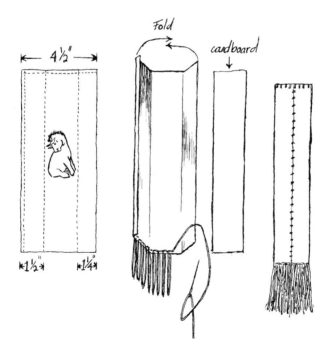

Outline Eeyore in small stitches in black wool.

Fill in the outline with larger stitches but shorter than ¼ inch. Give him a black mane and forelock.

Take a long piece of black wool. Knot the free end. At the bottom of the cloth, sew loops of wool, making the loops about 2½ to 3 inches long. Cut the bottom of the loops to make the fringe on Eeyore's tail.

Put the light cardboard back of Eeyore and between the lines.

Fold the cloth, lapping the 1½-inch edge over the 1¼-inch edge, and sew the upper edge down over the lower with simple ¼-inch stitches in wool.

You can also make these bookmarks out of paper by drawing Eeyore on the bookmark and drawing the fringe of his tail on the bottom. These are fine to use for Pin the Tail on Eeyore (see page 30).

Use them as prizes for the winners of the games you will play later or as favors. Make them before the party.

"Well, either a tail *is* there or it isn't there. You can't make a mistake about it. And yours *isn't* there!"
"Then what is?"
"Nothing."

Winnie-the-Pooh

POOH COLORING BOOK

paper, at least 8½″ × 11″   tracing paper
heavy thread and needle   pencil
rubber cement, paste, *or* glue   scissors

To make the book:

Take ten sheets of paper at least 8½ by 11 inches or larger, and fold them in half.

Sew along the fold in ½-inch stitches with strong thread. Knot the ends of the thread securely.

To make the outline drawings for coloring:

Trace or draw freehand pictures of your favorite Pooh characters and scenes from *Winnie-the-Pooh* and *The House at Pooh Corner*—one, two, or more on each page.

If you like, rubber cement, paste, or glue cardboard covers on the front and back pages. Cut the cardboard the same size as the paper.

If you make these beforehand as prizes or favors, letter on the front cover 1 to 2 inches down from the top:

A POOH COLORING BOOK
For: (*name of friend*)
(*Here draw a picture of Pooh and Eeyore*)
From: (*your name at the bottom*)

If you and some of your friends make them at the party, then just decorate them with drawings.

Draw pictures of any other Pooh characters on the back cover.

POOH MUSIC OR BOOK STAND

cardboard box as wide as an open book *or* a sheet of music, 1½"–2" deep	pencil scissors elastic bands

Take off the top of the box and put it down on a table. This is the holder for the stand.

Measure the two shorter sides of the bottom of the box to get the widest book or music stand.

Mark off the exact center on each.

Draw a line across the center from mark to mark and down the two sides.

Cut the sides in a narrow V up to the mark, and fold the bottom of the box along the pencil line.

Decorate the sides of the bottom of the box below the fold and the outside and inside of the top of the box with drawings—of Tigger and Pooh, Tigger and Eeyore, and Tigger and Piglet.

Stand the folded box bottom inside the box top.

Put one elastic band around either end of the folded bottom to make a book or music stand.

Put your copy of *The House at Pooh Corner* on the stand, open it to Chapter II, and hold it open with elastic bands to the pages you're working from.

This will make it easy for you to keep *Winnie-the-Pooh* and *The House at Pooh Corner* open to the drawings you want to use to decorate the things you make for the Pooh parties in this book.

Make an extra stand to use in the kitchen for this book, so that you can hold it open and upright to the recipe you're using.

Make a larger one for a friend or relative who could use a music stand.

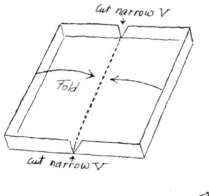

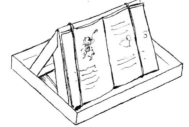

POOH MUSICAL INSTRUMENTS

DRUMS

cylindrical oatmeal,
   ice cream, *or* cornmeal box
rubber cement *or* glue
construction paper

scissors *or* knife
string, ribbon, *or* yarn
sticks *or* soup spoons

Use oatmeal, ice cream, or cornmeal boxes of different sizes to make several drums.

Take construction paper long enough to wrap around the cylinder box. If necessary, glue several pieces together.

Put the box on its side at one end of the paper. The top of the box should be even with the outside edge of the paper, as shown in the drawing.

Now roll the box across the paper and draw a line where the bottom rolls along the construction paper. Then roll it at least 1½ inches more than you need to cover the drum. Draw a line there.

Cut the paper along this line and down the other line you have drawn.

Draw, trace, or make silhouette pictures from the end papers (inside the cover) of *The House at Pooh Corner* on the construction paper.

Turn the paper over, so that the drawings will be on the outside of the drum when you roll the paper around it.

Punch a hole in the bottom of the box about ½ inch in from the edge.

Drape a piece of string, ribbon, or yarn long enough to go around your neck and cut it off, so that it hangs down to where you would like the drum to be—on or above your stomach.

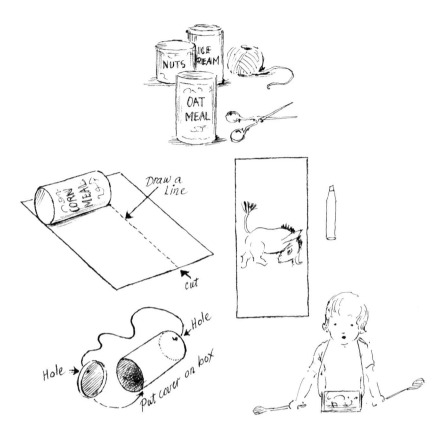

Tie a knot in one end of the string, ribbon, or yarn.

With the knot on the inside of the box, push the string through the hole and pull it until the knot stops it.

Remove the lid from the box.

Punch a hole in the lid the same distance from the edge as the hole in the bottom of the box.

Push the end of the string through the hole from the outside.

Knot it on the inside.

Put the lid back on the box and twist it around so that the string, ribbon, or yarn hangs evenly from both sides of the drum.

Brush a thin coat of rubber cement or glue on the plain side of construction paper.

Put the drum back on it and roll it across the paper, smoothing the paper from the decorated side onto the drum.

Paste the overlap down on the paper.

Hang the drum around your neck.

Use sticks or soup spoons as drumsticks.

At any party you will want to have more than one drummer, so make two or more.

"I shall sing that first line twice, and perhaps if I sing it very quickly, I shall find myself singing the third and fourth lines before I have time to think of them, and that will be a Good Song."

Winnie-the-Pooh

juice cans, empty, but with tops and bottoms
nut *or* coffee cans, empty, but with tin bottoms
    and plastic tops
anchor bottle opener *or* ice pick
string, ribbon, *or* yarn
chopsticks *or* knitting needles

To get drums with different tones, use large, empty juice, nut, or coffee cans of different sizes.

Make one hole in the top of a juice can with the anchor opener or ice pick near the rim.

Wash out the cans and let them stand over the sink, hole side down.

Put one hole in each of the plastic lids.

Now put a hole in the bottom of the can, opposite and the same distance from the rim as the hole in the top.

Run a string, ribbon, or length of yarn through the holes at each end of each can. The string, ribbon, or yarn should be the right length to hang, when knotted, around your neck and down to your stomach.

If you like, decorate them as you did the cylinder drums, or paint pictures directly on the cans.

Chopsticks or knitting needles make fine drumsticks and give different timbres to the drumming.

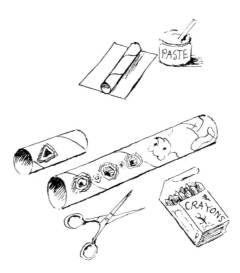

HUMMERS

cardboard rollers from household paper	scissors
	crayons

To make these, use as many rollers from rolls of any kind of household paper as you will have friends at your party.

If the rollers are white, decorate them with Pooh figures.

If they're gray, draw pictures on one side of a piece of construction paper and cover the rollers as you did the cylinder drums.

Punch three holes for notes, one under the other and ½ inch or more apart, along the tube.

Color around the note holes.

In addition to being good for humming through, they are good for singing and shouting through.

cardboard box, top *or* bottom, at least 10″ wide
elastic bands of different colors and widths

A harp is made the same way as a Pooh Music or Book Stand (see page 22) but with these two differences: you need only the top or bottom of a cardboard box; don't stand the harp inside the top of a box, but put many elastic bands of different widths and thicknesses and colors around it. Each rubber band will give a different note—Tiggerish and bouncy, perhaps.

Have a rhythm band at your party with you as the band leader. Give each guest an instrument to play. You may play to a recording or to radio music if you choose.

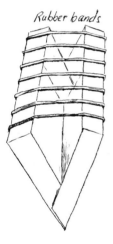

Rubber bands

So after breakfast they went round to see Piglet, and Pooh explained as they went that Piglet was a Very Small Animal who didn't like bouncing, and asked Tigger not to be too Bouncy just at first.

The House at Pooh Corner

Eeyore's birthday would not be properly celebrated unless you played this game.

Very good ready-made sets of Pin the Tail on the Donkey can be bought wherever toys are sold.

Of course you can make one for your Eeyore Birthday Party by drawing a tail-less Eeyore on a large sheet of wrapping paper. Make as many Eeyore Lost-Tail Bookmarks out of paper (see page 19) as you will have friends at your party. Put a pin in the top of each Bookmark.

Be sure to have a big handkerchief to use for blindfolding the players in turn. Remember to spin each player three times at the starting line before facing him toward Eeyore.

Whoever pins his Lost-Tail Bookmark closest to where Eeyore's tail should be is the winner.

Eeyore stood there, gazing sadly at the ground, and Winnie-the-Pooh walked all round him once.

"Why, what's happened to your tail?" he said in surprise.

"What *has* happened to it?" said Eeyore. "It isn't there!"

Winnie-the-Pooh

Choose a Safe-Home Line—the space between two trees, two big stones, two bushes, or two buildings.

Pick thistles (see page 14) to see who will be Eeyore.

Eeyore walks from the Safe-Home Line slowly, with the other players following him as close behind as they dare.

They call after Eeyore, "What time is it, Eeyore?"

Eeyore answers, "Nearly eleven o'clock," or any other time he chooses.

The other players continue to follow Eeyore and pester him for the time, faster and faster, "What's the time Eeyore?" "What's the time, Eeyore?"

Eeyore continues to walk slowly away from the Safe-Home Line, and answers with any "time" he thinks Eeyore would say, such as, "Thistle time," "Lost-Tail time."

But when Eeyore says, "Party time," the other players must turn and run for the Safe-Home Line, with Eeyore after them.

Whoever Eeyore catches first before reaching the Safe-Home Line is Eeyore for the next game.

"Dear, dear," said Pooh, "I didn't know it was as late as that."

Winnie-the-Pooh

POOH AND PIGLET TAG

Two friends are chosen by picking thistles (see page 14) to be Pooh and Piglet—the "Its."

Pooh and Piglet must hold hands and not let go as they chase the other players. If they let go, then they are "Its" for a second time.

Pooh and Piglet call out, "Run, run as fast as you can," and the other players start running. Pooh and Piglet, holding hands, run after them.

When all the players except one have been tagged, Pooh and Piglet let go hands until the last player is tagged.

The first and last players to be tagged are the "Its"—Pooh and Piglet—for the next round of the game.

"It's Pooh," said Christopher Robin excitedly.
"Possibly," said Eeyore.
"*And* Piglet!" said Christopher Robin excitedly.
"Probably," said Eeyore.

The House at Pooh Corner

MUSICAL POOH PILLOWS

If you don't have cushions or pillows enough, cut out some large round pieces of paper to use instead. Decorate them with Pooh characters. Have one fewer than there are players.

Put the pillows or paper seats on the floor in a straight line. Tape the paper seats to the floor. Allow enough room at either end of the line of pillows, so that the players can walk around them.

The players stand in an oval around the pillows.

You play one of the Musical Instruments that you have made before or earlier at the party—a drum, a hummer, or a harp.

When everybody is in line, you start to drum, hum, or strum. The players walk around the pillows. When you stop drumming, humming, or strumming, each player must find a pillow or paper seat to sit on. The player who is left standing is out of the game and must stand aside to watch.

If you like, the player who was left standing may play the musical instrument for the next round of the game, or you may both play an instrument. Decide on a signal beforehand for when you will stop playing.

Remove one of the paper seats or pillows.

The remaining players again stand in an oval around the remaining pillows, and the music begins again. When the drumming, humming, or strumming stops, the players must each find a pillow to sit on. The one who can't is out and stands aside to watch or becomes a third player of a musical instrument. Again, remove one pillow or paper seat.

And so the game continues until only one player—the winner—is left.

Players should walk, not run.

This game can also be played outdoors. Use stones instead of pillows or the round paper seats which you have made.

"He's going *round* and *round*," said Roo, much impressed.

"And why not?" said Eeyore coldly.

The House at Pooh Corner

II
A SPRING PARTY

And he began to wonder if all the other animals
would know that it was a special Pooh Party.

Winnie-the-Pooh

It was just the day for Organizing Something,
or for Writing a Notice Signed Rabbit.

The House at Pooh Corner

Invitations

Use writing paper, wrapping paper, or lightweight cardboard in spring colors.

Fold it in half.

Make sure it is a little smaller than the envelope it is to be mailed in.

Draw the outline of a large egg on the outside half of the invitation.

Draw Rabbit's ears or his head and ears, sticking over the top of the egg.

Print or write: COME TO MY SPRING PARTY and the name of a friend, inside the outline of the egg.

Open the invitation. On the inside page, print:

(the day)
(the time) from   o'clock to   o'clock

            (your name)
            (address)
            (telephone number)

Please let me know if you can come.
I hope you can.

Make one invitation for each friend you are inviting to your party and one extra in case later you remember somebody you have forgotten or in case you make a mistake.

Decorations

Use a plain white paper tablecloth, an old tablecloth, or an old clean sheet, big enough to cover the table.

Put it on the party table.

Draw a line on the tablecloth to mark the edge of the table.

Use tracings (see page 8 and pages 138–145) or draw Rabbit, Piglet, Pooh, Eeyore, and violets from Chapter V in *The House at Pooh Corner*. Put them just above the line marking the edge of the table and on the skirt of the cloth.

Use the same tracings or drawings on paper napkins.

Decorate paper plates and cups, too, several days beforehand, so the paint is dry. Do not serve hot food on painted paper plates.

It was going to be one of Rabbit's busy days. As soon as he woke up he felt important, as if everything depended upon him.

The House at Pooh Corner

PLACE CARDS

Print the name of each friend who will be at your party on the front of a napkin and put it at the place where he is to sit.

Or, print the name of a friend who will be at your party on a hard-boiled egg when you decorate it. Do names and decorations only in wax crayons of different colors. The colored wax crayon won't take the dye, and will keep its color. The eggshells will take the color of the dye.

Dye the eggs (see pages 40 and 41).

Put one at each place, so that your friends will know where you would like them to sit at the party table.

CENTERPIECE

Here are three ideas for centerpieces:

A glass bowl full of colored and decorated Easter eggs with or without the names of friends invited to the party printed on them before they're dyed. See page 41 for instructions on Dyes for Eggs.

Cut up yellow and green tissue paper in ¼-inch strips. Make a big nest of them for the center of the table. Fill the nest with colored Easter eggs.

A row of small bowls full of violets or other spring flowers down or around the center of the table with small nests of Easter eggs between the bowls.

Use wax crayons of white and of many colors. The white crayon will remain white when put in dye. The colored crayons will keep their color.

While the white-shelled eggs are boiling for 8 to 10 minutes to get hard, make tracings of Rabbit, Pooh, Piglet with violets, and of Eeyore as they are in Chapter V of *The House at Pooh Corner*. Use transparent paper and soft pencil.

Dry the eggs thoroughly.

Transfer the tracings of the drawings by putting the egg in an old towel crumpled up into a nest and holding the transparent paper against the egg, your fingers above and below the tracing.

Rub the back of the tracing back and forth with the soft pencil.

Color the tracing on the egg in wax crayon in appropriate colors.

If you can draw freehand, then don't make tracings but draw your pictures directly on the eggshell in crayon.

Write the names of Pooh characters on the eggs, one for each friend who will be at the party, along with the name of the friend.

These are the eggs to use for place cards and for the centerpiece.

He could spell his own name WOL, and he could spell Tuesday so that you knew it wasn't Wednesday.

The House at Pooh Corner

DYES FOR EGGS

White-shelled eggs work best, hard-boiled and dry.

Any packaged dyes are very good to use for coloring Easter eggs. But you can make dyes of your own from turmeric—the ingredient in curry that gives it its yellow color—from coffee, tea, onion skins, or a jar of violet blossoms. Experiment with other foods and spices yourself.

Be sure to draw or trace the Pooh pictures, decorations—of flowers, leaves, tracks, trees, or birds—and names on the eggs in wax crayon before dyeing. Any designs or printing you do on the eggs in wax crayon will *not* take dye. It's the uncrayoned eggshells that take the dye.

SPRING YELLOW DYE

1 heaping teaspoon turmeric   ¼ teaspoon vinegar
⅔ cup boiling water

Add the boiling water to the turmeric in a cup. Stir until turmeric is dissolved and add the vinegar.

BROWN DYES

1 heaping Tablespoon   ⅔ cup boiling water
   instant coffee   ½ teaspoon vinegar

Dissolve the coffee in the boiling water and add the vinegar. This gives a very nice rabbit brown.

2 teaspoons tea in a   *or*   2 tea bags
   tea strainer   ⅔ cup boiling water

Let the tea steep to a deep brown before dyeing the eggs. Tea makes a different brown from coffee.

ONION SKIN DYE

> outside skins of at least 2 onions,
> yellow, red, *or* both
2 cups water

Boil the eggs with the onion skins in the water slowly, for at
  least half an hour.

This will give you a color from pale yellow to a beautiful
  deep red, depending on the onion skins. The longer they
  sit, the deeper the color.

To get a stronger but still delicate onion taste, add a slice or
  two of raw onion to the onion skins before boiling.

VIOLET BLOSSOM DYES

If you live where violets grow or can buy a bunch in the
spring, wash them and fill a pint glass jar with the blossoms.

Violet-Blue: Cover the blossoms with the boiling water. Put
  the lid on the jar and let it sit for 24 hours. Strain off the
  violet-blue dye.

Lavender: To the violet-blue dye add the juice of 1 lemon
  and you will have a lavender or reddish-purple dye, depending on the violets.

Green: Add ¼ teaspoon of baking soda to the violet dye. It
  will turn green first and later yellow.

Things to Eat and Drink

HAM AND EGG LOAF

(Yield: about 12 ½" slices)

2 cups cold cooked ham,
diced
4 hard-boiled eggs, chopped
½ cup diced celery
¼ cup chopped scallion
or onion
2 radishes, diced (optional)
2 sprigs parsley, chopped
3–4 Tablespoons mayonnaise
salt (if necessary)
pepper (to taste)
1 8-oz. package cream
cheese

4–5 Tablespoons milk
¼ cup toasted sesame seeds
(optional)
1 1-lb. loaf of bread,
unsliced
mayonnaise (optional)
olives stuffed with
pimiento, sliced, *or*
thinly sliced rounds of
green pepper
sprigs of watercress *or*
parsley

Combine the ham, eggs, celery, scallion or onion, radishes,
and parsley.

Mix thoroughly and add the mayonnaise.

Add the salt, if necessary, and a grind or two of fresh pepper.

Soften the cream cheese with the milk until it will spread
as easily as cake frosting, and add the toasted sesame seeds,
if you like.

Cut off the top and side crusts of the bread.

Slice the loaf lengthwise so that you have three or four
layers.

Put the bottom layer on the serving platter and spread with
a thin coat of mayonnaise, if you like.

Spread with the ham and egg mixture to about ½ inch from the edges of the bread.

Cover the bottom layer with another bread layer and spread it with the ham and egg mixture.

Continue to the top layer of bread.

Press it down, so that the layers stick together.

Spread the loaf top and sides with the softened cream cheese.

Spell your name or Rabbit's in olive and green pepper slices. Underline the name with sprigs of watercress or parsley.

Slice from top to bottom to serve, about ½ inch thick, for approximately 12 servings.

RABBIT SALAD

spring lettuce, 1 large leaf *or* 2 small leaves for each guest	small sprig parsley
	small carrot, grated *or* chopped
¼ of 1 average-size scallion	salt
radish with leaves	freshly ground pepper

Wash all the salad ingredients, including the radish leaves.

Put the lettuce and radish leaves in paper towels to dry.

Wrap them in a damp towel and in plastic wrap. Refrigerate 2 or 3 hours before time to make the salad.

Dice the scallion and the parsley, and slice the radish.

Add these and the carrot to the salad just before dressing it.

Sprinkle on salt and pepper to taste.

This is good with or without salad dressing.

PIGLET UNDERNEATH CAKE

UNDERNEATH

(Preheat oven to 350° F.)

1 1-lb. can peach slices
   cherries; fresh, canned,
   or maraschino
½ cup slivered almonds
¼ cup (½ stick) butter
   or margarine

1 cup brown sugar
   large round cake pan at
   least 2″ deep *or* springform
   pan *or* 8–9″ iron frying pan

Pour off the juice from the peaches.

When the peaches are thoroughly drained, put six peach slices in the center of the pan and make circles of peaches around it until all the peaches are used.

Pit the cherries and cut them in half, or use the maraschino cherries, whole. Set them among the peaches in a pattern —a Pooh or Piglet pattern of your own invention.

Sprinkle it with the slivered almonds. You may use more than half a cup if you choose.

Melt the butter with the sugar in the pan.

Pour it over the peaches, cherries, and almonds.

"Underneath," said Piglet in an underneath sort of way.
"Underneath what?"
"You," squeaked Piglet. "Get up!"

The House at Pooh Corner

CAKE

⅓ cup, scant, butter
  or margarine
½ cup sugar
¼ cup honey
 2 eggs
1½ cups all-purpose
  unbleached flour

⅔ cup milk
 1 teaspoon powdered ginger
 3 teaspoons baking powder
¼ teaspoon baking soda
¼ teaspoon salt

Beat together the butter or margarine and sugar until creamy.

Add the honey.

Beat in the eggs, one at a time.

Sift the flour, ginger, baking powder, baking soda, and salt.

Add the flour mixture alternately with the milk, beginning and ending with the dry ingredients to give a finer texture to the cake.

Pour over the "Underneath" mixture and bake for 35 minutes.

Reduce heat to 300° F. and bake 20 minutes longer or until the cake springs back when touched in the center. If not done, turn heat down to 250° F. and bake 15 to 20 minutes longer.

Remove from oven and let cool.

When cool, run a knife or spatula around the edge. Put a flat cake serving dish over the cake pan and turn them both together, so that the "Underneath" is on top.

VIOLET HONEY SAUCE
FOR ICE CREAM OR CAKE

1–2 large bunches of violets
1 pint jar with lid
   boiling water
2 lemons, juiced
1 teaspoon water

1½ cups sugar
½ cup honey
2 Tablespoons cornstarch
   (optional)

If you live where violets grow, then you can make this de-
   licious Honey Sauce for cake and ice cream.
Wash the violets and remove the stems.
Pack the violet blossoms into the pint jar. Fill it full.
Cover the violet blossoms with boiling water and let stand
   for 24 hours.
Strain the violet water and add the lemon juice.
In a teaspoon of water over a low flame, mix the sugar and
   honey together until syrupy.
Add the violet water and lemon juice.
This is a delicious sauce which you can thicken with the
   cornstarch, over low heat, if you like.

But, as it happened, it was Rabbit
who saw Piglet first. Piglet had
got up early that morning to pick
himself a bunch of violets.

The House at Pooh Corner

VIOLET TEA WITH HONEY

This may be served hot or cold.

Make the violet tea exactly as you make the Violet Honey Sauce (page 47), except do not add the cornstarch and double the amount of water.

For *cold* Violet Tea, pour the hot violet tea over ice cubes in a glass or cup.

Float a violet or two on top. Drink with a straw.

"I think *Violets* are rather nice," said Piglet. And he laid his bunch in front of Eeyore and scampered off.

The House at Pooh Corner

Things to Make and Games to Play

BASKETS—FOR EASTER, MAY DAY,
EGG-COLLECTING, AND OTHER USES

brown paper bags, 14″ long, as many as you
    will have friends at your Spring Party
cardboard
crayons, felt-tipped pens, *or* paints
tape, paste, *or* glue
green and purple tissue paper

Let each friend cut a brown paper bag, folded, in half around the middle. Keep the top half.

Fold down the bottom half 1 inch from the top all the way around. Then fold it over and down another inch. This makes a cuff.

Re-crease the original creases in the corners to make them firm.

Decorate the cuff with drawings or tracings of Pooh and Piglet, violets and Eeyore, spring flowers and eggs.

". . . an ordinary biggish sort of basket, full of—"

The House at Pooh Corner

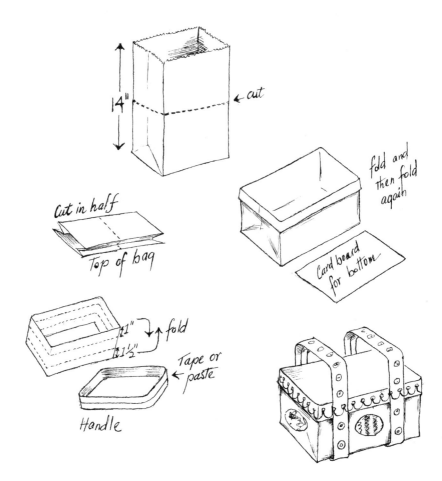

Color the sides of the bag in one color or in many colors or decorate them with a pattern in colors with crayons, felt-tipped pens, or paints.

Measure and cut a piece of cardboard exactly the size of the bottom of the bag by standing the bottom of the bag on the cardboard and tracing around it. (Greeting cards or last year's Christmas cards are very good for this.)

Fit the cardboard into the bottom of the bag.

Fold the top half of the bag, which you kept, in half around the middle.

Cut it on the fold.

Fold each half in from each edge about 1 inch toward the middle, so that you have folded edges on the outer edges of both handles. Fold one edge ½ inch deeper in than the other.

Turn the handles inside out, so the cut edges are outside.

Tape, paste, or glue the wider cut edge over the narrower.

Turn the handles right side out.

Color them the same as the basket.

Slip the basket about 1 inch or so inside one handle and tape, paste, or glue it, bottom and sides, to the basket. Attach the other handle in the same way.

TISSUE-PAPER STRAW

Cut the green and purple tissue paper into ¼-inch strips.

You can make a lot of tissue paper straw at one time by folding the tissue paper in half and then in half again before cutting it. Line the basket with it.

Besides being good for holding Easter eggs and flowers for May Day, these baskets are also good for taking on Expotitions or Organized Searches, and for Easter Egg Hunts. They will each hold a sandwich, a carrot, a piece of fruit, a cookie, and a paper napkin nicely. They are also good work baskets.

EGG DECORATION AND DYEING

This is a good thing for you and your friends to do at your Spring Party. Be sure you say on the invitation that your friends should wear clothes they won't mind getting wet or stained with vegetable dye.

Boil enough white-shelled eggs so that each friend at your party will be able to draw designs on and to dye at least two eggs.

Follow the directions given on pages 40 and 41.

These can go in the Basket (see page 49), which each guest will take home.

For the spring is really springing;
You can see a skylark singing,
And the blue-bells, which are ringing,
  Can be heard.

The House at Pooh Corner

EGG HUNT

This is a game to play after you and your friends have each made a Basket (page 49).

The day before the party, put the names of the friends who will be at the party and pictures of Rabbit and other Pooh characters or designs on hard-boiled eggs. See Designs for Easter Eggs (page 40).

Do four eggs for each friend.

The day of the party, hide the eggs indoors or out, depending on where you live and where you will have the party. Be sure to put some eggs near the ground or the floor for friends who are short, and others, in higher places, for friends who are tall.

Whoever finds the most eggs wins.

After all the eggs have been found (count them to be sure), each guest takes home in his basket the four eggs with his or her name on them.

He didn't know whether he ought to be looking for Small at the top of an oak-tree or in the petal of a buttercup.

The House at Pooh Corner

Let each friend at the party choose the Pooh character he would like to be for this race—whichever character he thinks would run the fastest. If you have more friends at your party than there are Pooh characters, then there can be two or more of any character.

Give each player a hard-boiled egg, and line the players up on a mark which they must toe.

When the players are lined up, holding a hard-boiled egg, you call out,

> One for the money,
> Two for the prize,
> Three to get ready,
> And four is—OFF.

At the word, "OFF," each player rolls his hard-boiled egg, as he would a bowling ball, on the grass, ground, or floor. He stands still until his egg stops rolling.

As soon as his egg stops rolling, the player runs to it, picks it up, and rolls it again.

Each player tries to roll his egg for the last roll, just to the finish line or beyond.

Whoever reaches the finish line first is the winner.

"Is Piglet organdized too?"
"We all are," said Rabbit, and off he went.

The House at Pooh Corner

III

A PICNIC, SWIMMING, AND EXPOTITION PARTY

"Going on an Expotition?" said Pooh eagerly.
"I don't think I've ever been on one of those.
Where are we going to on this Expotition?"

Winnie-the-Pooh

"Expedition, silly old Bear.
It's got an 'x' in it."

Winnie-the-Pooh

Invitations

This is a good kind of party to have to celebrate the end of school, a birthday in summer, or going back to school.

Draw the shape of a picnic basket on a piece of colored paper or brown wrapping paper.

On the front of the basket write:

> *(name of friend you are inviting)*,
> please come to a Picnic, Swimming, and
> Expotition Party. Bring your bathing suit
> and towel. Wear clothes to play in.
>
> The party will be on *(day and date)*
> from   o'clock to   o'clock.
>
> Please let me know that you can come.
>
> > *(your name)*
> > *(address)*
> > *(telephone number)*

If you live where there's no beach or pond or brook or river or pool, then leave out "Swimming" in the invitation to your party and don't ask your friends to bring their bathing suits. There are lots of other things to discover in the city and the country. You could, for instance, also discover a pond or a lake or a brook or a river, a playground where you've never been, a beach, a wooded place.

Decorations

TABLECLOTH AND NAPKINS, PAPER PLATES AND CUPS

Decorate the picnic tablecloth and napkins on a rainy day, a week or two before the picnic party.

Use a clean old sheet or a plain paper tablecloth as a picnic cloth to put on the ground.

Draw freehand or trace pictures from Pooh and His Friends in this book (pages 138–145), from Chapter VIII of *Winnie-the-Pooh*, or from Chapters V and VI of *The House at Pooh Corner* onto the tablecloth and on the paper napkins, plates, and cups.

In addition to pictures of Piglet and Pooh, Eeyore and Christopher Robin, Kanga and Roo, Owl and Rabbit and Tigger, you may want to use pictures of bees and butterflies, dandelions and thistles, which are all in *Winnie-the-Pooh*. Put the name of each friend on a paper cup, so that he can use it more than once.

On the day of the party, cut a hole in the center of the tablecloth big enough for the North Pole. The North Pole can be made of a mop or broom handle or a good-sized stick.

Use a side of a cardboard carton for the sign that is to go on your North Pole. Of course, you may want to discover the South Pole or the East and West Poles or a Very Special Spot in a park where you live. Letter on your sign whatever is appropriate for your party.

Attach the sign to the Pole as you see it in this picture.

Put the Pole through the hole in the tablecloth and stick it in the ground. If necessary, everybody can gather stones to prop up the Pole. At the beach, stick the Pole in the sand.

Weight down the edges of the tablecloth and paper napkins with stones or shells.

"Oh!" said Pooh again. "What *is* the North Pole?" he asked.

"It's just a thing you discover," said Christopher Robin.

Winnie-the-Pooh

DECORATED TOWELETTES
FOR WASHING AND DRYING

To decorate packaged moistened towelettes for washing,
cut pieces of colored paper larger than the envelope the
towelette comes in and large enough so that you can draw
pictures from Chapter VIII of *Winnie-the-Pooh* on the top
half and write the name of a friend who will be at your
party. Do one towelette for each friend.

Paste or tape each packaged towelette to the bottom of the
paper. Put them in various places on the tablecloth.

Decorate plain paper towels with some of the same tracings or drawings that you used on the tablecloth and paper
napkins.

Things to Eat and Drink

HONEY BREAD

(Preheat oven to 350° F.)

2 cups all-purpose flour	½ cup liquid honey
1 teaspoon baking powder	1 egg
1 teaspoon baking soda	1 cup milk
1 teaspoon salt	butter *or* margarine
½ teaspoon ground cinnamon	loaf pan
1 teaspoon ground ginger	

Butter a loaf pan.
Butter the inside of a measuring cup. Pour in the honey.
Sift and measure the flour.

"And the only reason for being a bee
that I know of is making honey."

Winnie-the-Pooh

Sift in the baking powder, soda, salt, cinnamon, and ginger, and sift twice more.

Beat the egg, gradually adding the milk.

Add the egg and milk mixture to the dry ingredients alternately with the honey.

Beat well and pour the mixture into the loaf pan.

Bake about 45 minutes, until golden on top.

If the bread is done, the loaf will come out of the pan easily when you tap it all around and turn the pan over.

If it is not done, put it back in the oven for another 10 to 15 minutes.

Cool on a rack.

Slice and butter when cool, which makes very good bread-and-butter sandwiches, with or without a teaspoon of honey.

This should be made the day before your Picnic Party.

"Yes," he said, "it is. No doubt about that. And honey, I should say, right down to the bottom of the jar. Unless, of course," he said, "somebody put cheese in at the bottom just for a joke."

Winnie-the-Pooh

CHEDDAR CHEESE BREAD

(Preheat oven to 375° F.)

¼ cup (½ stick) butter
  or margarine
2 cups all-purpose flour
4 teaspoons baking powder
½ teaspoon salt

2 cups (½ lb.) shredded
  Cheddar cheese
2 eggs
1 cup milk
loaf pan

Butter the loaf pan.

Melt the butter or margarine.

Sift and measure the flour.

Sift twice more after adding the baking powder and salt.

Add the cheese.

Beat the eggs and add the milk as the eggs froth.

Stir the egg-milk mixture into the dry mixture and beat enough to blend.

Stir in the melted butter.

Pour into the loaf pan.

Bake for 40 minutes. When the loaf has shrunk from the sides of the pan and is golden on top, it is usually done.

Tap the bottom of the pan. If the loaf comes out easily, it is done. If it is not done, return it to the oven and bake longer. When done, remove from the pan, and cool immediately.

This tastes just as fresh and good if it is made the day before the party.

BREADPLATE SANDWICHES

Make cheese bread by using the recipe for Cheddar Cheese
   Bread (see page 63). Shape it in small, round loaves and
   bake the loaves in small, round pans.
Bake them for a shorter time than you do the regular loaves.
Set out an assortment of Sandwich Spreads (see page 65),
   cold meats, cheeses, and Fruit Juice Butters (see page
   66), whichever you like, in bowls and on platters.
When you are ready to eat, cut the loaves around the mid-
   dle instead of from top to bottom.
Let each friend make his own breadplate sandwich.

He looked round at them in his
melancholy way. "I suppose none
of you are sitting on a thistle by
any chance?"

Winnie-the-Pooh

SANDWICH SPREADS

CREAM CHEESE OR COTTAGE CHEESE

The same ingredients in the same proportions may be added to a 3-ounce package of cream cheese, softened with a little milk, or to 8 ounces of cottage cheese.

All these sandwich spreads may be made the day before the party and refrigerated until ready to use.

½ average-size carrot, finely chopped

3 watercress *or* mastershalum leaves, in season

Remove the stems. Wash the leaves. Cut the mastershalum leaves in pieces; watercress leaves may be left whole.

Stir leaves and chopped carrot into the softened cream or cottage cheese.

½ cup diced pineapple *or* other fruit cut in small pieces: cherries, peaches,

apricots, nectarines, bananas, whole berries

Stir until thoroughly mixed into the cheese.

1 Tablespoon honey
1 teaspoon orange juice

1 teaspoon finely grated orange rind

Soften the cream cheese with the honey and orange juice. Add the orange rind and mix thoroughly.

2 Tablespoons each, finely diced cucumber and celery

1 Tablespoon each, diced scallion, radish, and carrot

Stir the vegetables into the cheese and stir until well mixed.

FRUIT JUICE BUTTERS FOR UNEXPECTED SANDWICHES

1 cup (2 sticks) butter *or* margarine
3 Tablespoons juice: orange, lemon, lime,
   pineapple, apricot, peach, cherry, pear,
   raspberry, strawberry, *or* any other

Let the butter or margarine stand at room temperature
   until soft.
Add 3 Tablespoons of fruit juice to 1 cup of butter or margarine and let it stand in a covered jar overnight in a
   cool place.
Pour off any juice not absorbed and spread fruit juice butters on slices of bread for sandwiches.

"Have you all got something?" asked
Christopher Robin with his mouth full.

Winnie-the-Pooh

FRUIT BASKET

Wash an assortment of whatever fruits are in season. Be
sure they are ripe.

Dry them well.

Do not refrigerate. Cold fruit never has as much taste as
fruit at room temperature.

Arrange the fruit in as wide a picnic basket as possible, so
that they will not sit on top of each other and be bruised.

NORTH POLE DESSERT:
COCONUT SNOWBALLS

shredded coconut
vanilla ice cream
plastic bags
ice cream scoop

ice cream cones *or*
cups and spoons
red and blue food coloring
(optional)

Fill a small bowl with shredded coconut.

Dip out two scoops of vanilla ice cream for each friend at the party.

With a big tablespoon, roll the ice cream balls around in the coconut.

Pop each one into a plastic sandwich bag and all the sandwich bags into a larger plastic bag.

Return to the freezer and let them stay overnight.

Take them to the picnic in a cooler with ice on top.

Take along ice cream cones and the scoop or put the snowballs in a cup and give each friend a spoon to eat them with.

If you like, color the coconut lavender by mixing red and blue food coloring. In that case, you will have made Thistle Snowballs, which you can also serve at An Eeyore Birthday Party (see page 10) .

So off they all went to discover the Pole.
Winnie-the-Pooh

Leave all food scraps and crumbs on the ground where they
fall, so that Henry Rush, Alexander Beetle, Smallest of All,
and Rabbit's other friends and relations can have a feast
after you leave the picnic.

Put all other things—used paper plates, towels, napkins,
cups—in a public trash basket or take them home to put in
one of your own.

And all Rabbit's friends-and-relations
spread themselves about on the grass,
and waited hopefully in case anybody
spoke to them, or dropped anything, or
asked them the time.

Winnie-the-Pooh

Things to Make and Games to Play

HAYCORN, NUT, SHELL,
AND STONE FACES

stones *or* shells	pipe cleaners
haycorns *or* other nuts	colored paper
buttons and beads	pail
pieces of fur, real or fake	scissors
pieces of cloth and felt	crayons, felt-tipped pens,
short lengths of yarn,	*or* paints
ribbon, braid, and string	rubber cement *or* glue

After lunch, in the hour before you can all go swimming again or are ready to play games, everybody can help gather a pail full of stones or shells. If you live where there are oak trees, perhaps you can bring along some acorns. If not, bring along large nutshells. Stones with one flat surface are best. Large shells are easier to work with than small ones.

Let each friend take one, two, or more nuts, stones, or shells. The shapes will probably suggest Pooh characters.

Bring along on the picnic a basket of assorted odds and ends of the kind listed above—buttons, beads, etc.

Besides these odds and ends, have two or three crayons, felt-tipped pens, or paints of different colors and several small tubes of glue or rubber cement.

Now let everybody sit in a circle around the equipment and put faces on the stones, shells, and nuts—faces of Pooh and Piglet, Owl and Rabbit, Eeyore and Tigger, Kanga and Roo. Or Christopher Robin.

Or make a bee with a small stone. Color it black with yellow stripes. Paste on black wings and feelers, legs and feet.

Or make Small—black with orange spots.

These make good paperweights for a desk or work table. At a picnic, they can weight down the tablecloth and napkins on a breezy day—and anything else that might blow away.

A POOH TREASURE HUNT

You can have a hunt for Treasure hidden at the NORTH POLE by using the map inside the covers of *Winnie-the-Pooh* for laying out the route of your Treasure Hunt in your yard, in a wooded place, or in a park.

Make cardboard signs of the places on the map and as many copies of the map as you will have friends at the party. Number the places on the map.

The morning of the party, lay out the route, and hide the signs along it in the same order as the places on the map, beginning with MY HOUSE or EEYORES GLOOMY PLACE as spot number 1 and going on around to the NORTH POLE.

Divide your friends into two teams or let each friend hunt alone. Give each friend a map. Using the map, each team or each "hunter" tries to find the spot where you have hidden each sign. The signs must be found in numerical order.

The team or hunter who reaches the NORTH POLE first wins.

If some of the players can't read, number the cardboard signs and draw the same picture on each as the one on the map, but a little larger.

The winning team or hunter is served the "Treasure" first—Coconut Snowballs (see page 68) from a picnic cooler in ice cream cones or in cups to be eaten with spoons.

If you're very clever and you and your friends can read very well, instead of signs and pictures use only clues. The clues should be quotations from *Winnie-the-Pooh* or *The House at Pooh Corner* which describe the places on the map and the place where you have actually hidden the next clue. Number each written clue in the same order as on the map and your route.

"It's—I wondered—It's only—
Rabbit, I suppose *you* don't know,
What does the North Pole *look* like."
"Well," said Rabbit, stroking
his whiskers. "Now you're asking me."

Winnie-the-Pooh

This is a game that can be played in shallow water, on the beach, in a yard, or in a park.

If you play it in the water, the players may not go beyond a certain depth. Anyone who does is out of the game.

If you play it on land, then mark the boundaries by stones, bushes, trees, or other objects.

Choose one friend to be Pooh. Pooh is "It."

Pooh calls out, "Piglet."

The other players scatter around the playing area or in shallow water. When Pooh calls, "Piglet," the other players answer, "Pooh."

Pooh calls "Piglet" constantly and at the same time moves toward a player who just as constantly answers, "Pooh."

All the players *must* answer "Pooh" when Pooh calls "Piglet."

Pooh tries to catch a player. The player he catches becomes Pooh.

The winner is the player who never is caught, or caught the fewest number of times.

"Pooh, did you see me swimming?
Hallo, Piglet! I say, Piglet!
What do you think I was doing!
Swimming!"

Winnie-the-Pooh

THE ALEXANDER BEETLE GAME

pail and shovel
5 shells, pebbles, *or* buttons, one set
   for each friend who will play the game
crayons, felt-tipped pens, *or* paints

Dig an Alexander Beetle hole in the sand or dirt or use a small plastic pail or pan.

Give each friend 5 shells, pebbles, or buttons, each set marked with a color or a letter or in some way to make it different from the others.

Draw a toe-line.

Each friend takes a turn tossing his shells, pebbles, or buttons from the toe-line into the Alexander Beetle hole.

The one who gets the most shells, pebbles, or buttons in the hole wins.

And the last and smallest friend-and-
relation was so upset to find that
the whole Expotition was saying "Hush!"
to *him,* that he buried himself head
downwards in a crack in the ground. . . .
His name was Alexander Beetle.

Winnie-the-Pooh

Choose one player to be Christopher Robin. He will be the caller. He turns his back to the players.

The players each choose the name of a Pooh character and line up at the starting mark.

With his back to the players, Christopher Robin calls out the name of each Pooh character in turn. And each player answers in turn, "How many steps to the Top of the Forest?"

Christopher Robin answers, "Take two Christopher Robin steps," or he might answer, "So-and-so many Pooh or Piglet steps," or "So-and-so many Rabbit hops, Kanga or Roo hops, Tigger leaps, Owl wings-dips, or Alexander Beetle crawls."

Before the player takes the step, hop, leap, wing-dip, or crawl he has been told to take, he must ask, "May I?" If he forgets the "May I?" he must go back to the starting line and begin over again on his next turn.

So they went off together. But wherever they go, and whatever happens to them on the way, in that enchanted place on the top of the Forest, a little boy and his Bear will always be playing.

The House at Pooh Corner

There are two ways to end Pooh-Steps and get a winner. One, the winner is the player who reaches Christopher Robin first and touches him on the back. Or two, the player who reaches Christopher Robin first, touches him on the back; then Christopher Robin and all the players turn and run for the starting line. The player who is not caught by Christopher Robin and reaches the starting line first is the winner.

The winner becomes Christopher Robin for the next round of the game.

Be sure to decide beforehand how long or short the steps, hops, leaps, wing-dips, and crawls are to be.

POOH STATUES

The player chosen to be the "Spinner" and the "Judge" of the Pooh Statues takes one player at a time by the hand. He stands in the center and spins the other player around him in a circle several times.

As he spins each player, he chants,

> 3 cheers for Pooh!
> (For Who?)
> For You—
> (Why, what did I do?)
> I thought you knew—
> Be (*name of a Pooh character*) or Pooh.

In the last line of the chant, the Spinner calls out the name of a Pooh character and lets go of the player's hand.

The player spins away, and as he slows down, takes a pose—like a statue—of the character he has been told to be or of Pooh.

If the character the player is to be is Owl, then he might have his arms out like wings, ready to flap; if Eeyore, he might be on the ground, looking to see if he has a tail; if Piglet, he might be smelling violets; if Pooh, he'd be eating honey or have his head in a honey jar.

The Spinner is also the Judge of the statues. He looks them all over. The one he judges to look most like the Pooh character he is supposed to be, or like Pooh, is the winner.

IV
A HONEY-TASTING
PARTY FOR POOH

"A party for me?" thought Pooh
to himself. "How grand!"

Winnie-the-Pooh

"Well, it's a very nice pot, even if there's no honey in it."

Winnie-the-Pooh

Invitations

Make a pattern of a honey pot out of heavy paper or light-weight cardboard, a little smaller than the envelope you will send the invitations in.

Lay the pattern on the side of a small, brown, folded paper bag. The paper bag must be the kind with a flat, not rounded, bottom.

Put the bottom of the honey pot on one bottom crease of the paper bag.

Draw around it.

Cut it out on the two sides and the top. Not the bottom. Leave the bottom folded.

Make as many of these as you will need invitations.

On the outside of the honey pot in different-colored crayons write:

Please Come to My
Honey-Tasting Party
on *(day)*, the *(date)*
from   o'clock to   o'clock

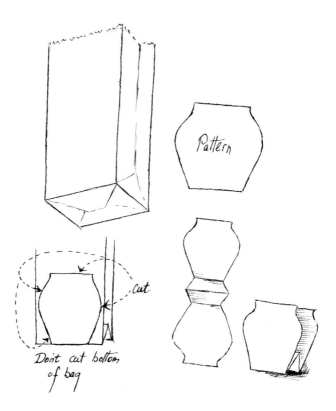

On the inside of the invitation write in crayon:

Come in costume as Pooh or Piglet, Eeyore or Rabbit, Owl or Tigger, Kanga or Roo, or Christopher Robin —or even Alexander Beetle or Smallest of All.

I hope you can come. Please let me know.

(*your name*)
(*address*)
(*telephone number*)

On the outside of the back of the honey pot, write HUNNY in big letters.

Decorations

TABLECLOTH AND NAPKINS

Decorate a paper tablecloth and napkins with any pictures of Pooh tasting or eating honey. Draw them freehand or trace them.

You could also add a few leaves and fir cones. Draw them as a border around the tablecloth and on the napkins—bigger ones on the tablecloth; smaller ones on the napkins.

If you live near a park or in the country where you can pick up autumn leaves, paste them on your tablecloth and napkins.

Or you can make table mats of heavy wrapping paper in honey-pot shapes, decorated with leaves and pictures of Pooh tasting honey.

"Owl," said Christopher Robin, "I am going to give a party."

Winnie-the-Pooh

POTS FOR HONEY-TASTING

If you can get a small honeycomb or two from a beekeeper in your neighborhood or from a specialty food store *and* some honey of unusual flavors, such as wild blueberry, wild rose, thyme, lime blossom—or honey from foreign countries —get some for the honey-tasting at your party.

Honey keeps well. Put the honeycombs in plastic bags and use tie-arounds to keep them airtight. Keep them in a cool place but not in the refrigerator or they will crystallize.

Save up some small bottles—plastic pill bottles, carefully washed out, are very good—and put different flavors of honey in different bottles. Have bottles enough, so that each friend at the party can take home a sample of a special honey.

Label each bottle and write on it the name of the friend who is to take it home from your party.

These go in the big honey pot in the center of your party table.

Have plenty of plastic spoons on hand for the friends at your party to taste the different honeys.

BLUE AND GREEN BALLOONS

Use blue and green balloons of all sizes and shapes as decorations.

Outdoors: Hang them by strings tied around the mouths of the balloons from shrubs and from tree branches.

Indoors: Hang them in clusters around the room where you will have the party—from a chandelier in the dining room, in the corners of the room, and wherever else it is possible and appropriate.

CENTERPIECE

Use honey pots and honeycombs in a big honey pot made out of a basket or hatbox, covered in brown paper.

Tie balloons to the big honey pot. Stand the big honey pot on a bed of leaves on the table. If you have no real leaves, cut leaves out of colored paper—yellow, red, green, and brown.

Give the little honey pots to your guests when it's time to do the honey-tasting at the party.

"When you go after honey with a balloon, the great thing is not to let the bees know you're coming."

Winnie-the-Pooh

Things to Eat and Drink

WAFFLEWITCHES
WITH APPLE NUT SALAD

3 cups waffle mix *or*
  packaged frozen waffles
1 cup grated American
  cheese
¼ cup mayonnaise
3 Tablespoons minced
  scallion

1 Tablespoon minced
  parsley
¼ cup diced celery
1 cup cooked chicken *or*
  turkey, diced
1 teaspoon fresh thyme *or*
  ½ teaspoon dried thyme
  salt and pepper (to taste)

Prepare the waffle mix and bake on your waffle iron according to the directions on the package. This will make fifty 3-inch waffles or enough for twenty-five wafflewitches. Or use packaged frozen waffles.

Combine all the other ingredients and let them sit while you bake the waffles.

Spread the wafflewitch filling on one waffle and top with another.

These may be made ahead of time, wrapped in foil, and kept in a warming oven at the lowest temperature until ready to serve.

APPLE NUT SALAD

For each serving, allow:
¼ eating apple, peeled
  and diced
  a few raisins

1 Tablespoon nutmeat
  pieces: walnuts, pecans,
  or cashews
1 lettuce leaf cup

SALAD DRESSING

For 8 to 10 salads, allow:

6 Tablespoons vegetable *or* peanut oil	dash of pepper, freshly ground
2 Tablespoons cider vinegar	1 Tablespoon honey
1 teaspoon salt	

Combine the salad ingredients, except the lettuce.
Mix the honey with the oil and vinegar dressing.
Pour the dressing over the salad ingredients and mix.
Spoon the salad ingredients into the lettuce leaves.
Serve.

So now let's give him three hearty cheers
(*So now let's give him three hearty whiches?*)
And hope he'll be with us for years and years,
And grow in health and wisdom and riches!
3 Cheers for Pooh!

Winnie-the-Pooh

BLACK CLOUD HONEY CAKE
WITH WALNUT BEES

CAKE

(Preheat oven to 350° F.)

8 plain chocolate bars, ⅞-oz. size	2½ cups all-purpose flour
	¼ teaspoon salt
1 cup (2 sticks) butter *or* magarine	½ teaspoon baking soda
	¼ cup buttermilk
1 cup honey	grated rind of 1 orange
1 cup sugar	*or* 1 lemon
4 eggs	tube pan
2 5½-oz. cans chocolate syrup	

Melt the chocolate bars in the top of a double boiler.

Cream the butter, honey, and sugar until the butter absorbs the honey and sugar.

Add the eggs, one at a time. Beat vigorously after adding each egg.

Add the chocolate syrup, beating as you pour it in.

Sift the flour, salt, and soda together and add it alternately with the buttermilk to the mixture to get a cake of fine texture.

Add the melted chocolate bars to the cake batter and the orange or lemon rind. Beat.

Fill a tube pan half full and bake for 1 hour or until a cake tester or a knife comes out clean from the middle of the cake.

ICING

1 lb. confectioners' sugar	½ cup (1 stick) butter,
½ cup cocoa	softened
1 teaspoon honey	6 Tablespoons milk
6 Tablespoons milk	⅛ teaspoon salt
	walnut halves

Mix all ingredients (except walnut halves) together in the top of a double boiler over simmering water, and stir until icing will spread easily.

Remove from heat and cool 5 minutes. If too liquid, add a little confectioners' sugar; if too thick, add milk.

Ice cake. Reserve 1 Tablespoon of icing.

Decorate with walnut halves in a pattern of flying bees.

Make bees' heads with dots of icing, using the Tablespoon of icing that you have reserved.

"You never can tell with bees." He thought
for a moment and said: "I shall try to
look like a small black cloud. That will
deceive them."

Winnie-the-Pooh

HONEY DOUGHNUTS

4 cups all-purpose flour	1 cup sugar
2 teaspoons cream of tartar	1 cup sour milk
1 teaspoon salt	1½ teaspoons melted
1½ teaspoons baking soda	margarine *or* shortening
¼ teaspoon grated	vegetable oil *or* lard for
cinnamon	frying
1 teaspoon grated nutmeg	bowls of different kinds
1 large egg	of honey, if you like
1 Tablespoon honey	

Sift the flour, cream of tartar, salt, soda, cinamon, and nutmeg into a bowl.

In a second bowl, beat the egg and add the honey, sugar, sour milk, and melted margarine or shortening.

Add the dry ingredients a little at a time to the egg mixture. Mix thoroughly.

Flour a pastry board or wax paper which you may use to cover the pastry board.

Flour the rolling pin and roll out the dough ¼ inch thick. Cut with a doughnut cutter.

They were just going to argue about it, when Piglet remembered that, if they put acorns in the Trap, *he* would have to find the acorns, but if they put honey, then Pooh would have to give up some of his own honey.

Winnie-the-Pooh

Vegetable Oil or Lard for Frying

Use enough vegetable oil or lard to fill your pan ½ to ⅔ full. Be sure the pan is big enough to hold a wire basket for deep-fat frying. Or use an electric frying pan set at 375° F.

The vegetable oil must be kept at 370° F. on a thermometer for liquids, often called a candy thermometer. If you do not have such a thermometer, test the temperature of your oil by dropping a 1-inch cube of bread into it. If it browns in 1 minute, the oil or lard is the right temperature for cooking your doughnuts.

Now put your doughnuts in the wire basket and into the pan. Drop them into the fat in the electric frying pan. Fry first on one side and then the other. Turn them with a long-handled fork.

Drain on brown paper covered with paper towels.

Serve a doughnut to each guest. Ask him to break it in quarters. Let each guest dip each quarter of his doughnut in a different kind of honey.

HONEY CLOVE CIDER

| 1 orange, thinly sliced | 1 gallon pure cider |
| whole cloves | 1 cup honey |

Slice the orange in ¼-inch slices, and cut each slice in
quarters.
Stick a clove in each quarter.
Pour the cider into a large pan.
Heat but do not boil.
Add the honey and stir until well blended.
Pour into a punch or serving bowl.
Float the orange slices with the cloves on top of the cider.
Serve warm.

Instead of slicing the oranges, stick 2 whole ones, which you
have washed and dried, with 10 or more cloves.
Put the oranges on a flat pan to heat for about half an hour
in a 300° F. oven.
Proceed as above while the oranges are baking.

But Pooh went back to his
own house, and feeling
very proud of what he had
done, had a little something
to revive himself.

Winnie-the-Pooh

PUMPKIN SEEDS

(Preheat oven to 200° F.)

seeds from a pumpkin   screw-top jars
salt

A day or two before your Honey-Tasting Party, cut the top
   off a pumpkin and scrape out the seeds.
Pull out the pumpkin strings.
Wash the seeds to remove the remaining pumpkin strings.
Dry them on paper towels.
Put the seeds, not touching, on a shallow pan.
Let them roast to a delicate golden color for about 1 hour.
Remove from the oven and while still hot, sprinkle with
   salt.
Eat a few yourself. Hot or cold they taste like nuts.
Spoon the rest into the clean screw-top jars and store for the
   party.

"It's a very difficult thing,
planting, unless you know
how to do it," he said.

The House at Pooh Corner

GRAPES TO RAISINS

Use any kind of grapes. Different sizes take different lengths
of time to dry out.

Wash the grapes and drain off as much water as you can.

Cut them into as many small bunches as you will have
friends at your Honey-Tasting Party, or remove them
singly from their stems.

Distribute the grapes in bunches or singly on a flat baking
pan.

Put them in a 170° F. oven for 5 to 6 hours.

Turn them often.

They should be moist dry.

Another way to make raisins is to dry the grapes over several
days by putting them in an oven which has begun to cool
after you have baked cakes or roasted pumpkin seeds. Be
sure the oven is not hotter than 200° F. before you put
the grapes in it or they will char.

And he looked up at the ceiling
with his head on one side, and
made exploring noises with his
tongue and considering noises,
and what-have-we-got-*here* noises.

The House at Pooh Corner

Things to Make and Games to Play

PAPER BAG MASKS

brown paper bags	scissors
pencils, crayons, paints	heavy wool for hair
or felt-tipped pens	glue *or* needle and thread

Give each friend at your party a brown paper bag, big enough to fit over his or her head.

Fold the bottom of the bag in half along the center so that the two halves are back to back.

Let each friend draw the head of his favorite Pooh character, or the head of the character he's dressed as, on the front of the paper bag—face and ears. Use the bottom of the paper bag as the top of the mask.

Cut along the inside lines of the ears and the top of the head. For Rabbit's ears, staple or pin the inside edge in one place to help them stand.

Do not cut the sides of the face or ears. If you do, you will then have a face mask and not one that fits over the head.

Open up the paper bag.

Cut out the eyes, nose, and mouth.

The bag masks can be worn as they are. They can also be colored with crayons, felt pens, or paints and used at a holiday party or as wall decorations.

Here is another kind of mask you and your friends can make.

Cut off the bottoms of a brown paper bag so that the paper bag from bottom to top fits comfortably over the head and neck, to the shoulders.

Fold bottom of bag up

Cut out eyes, nose and mouth

Lightly mark the bag where the mouths, noses, and eyes should go with a crayon. Cut them out.

Make ears and glue them on.

Use heavy wool for hair and sew or glue it on.

Feathers for Owl and stripes for Tigger can be done in crayon, felt pen, or paint.

THE POOHSTICK GAME

This is a good outdoors game.

Use real sticks for this if you live where you can throw sticks from a bridge into the water. Begin by gathering a pile of sticks, so that each friend has five. Mark each set with different color paint.

Let each friend throw one stick from one side of the bridge into the water.

Then, as in Chapter VI of *The House at Pooh Corner,* run to the other side of the bridge to see whose stick comes out from under the bridge first. The winner is the one who has the most sticks come out first from under the bridge.

Or, if there isn't a bridge, choose a rock or log or some natural target in the brook or pond or lake or river, and let the players try to hit it. Whoever hits it or hits closest, wins.

If you live where this game can't be played, fill a pail or a tub—even a bathtub—with water and let the players take turns throwing sticks into the pail or tub.

Stand the pail on newspaper, plastic, or foil.

Put down a piece of paper to show the line from which the players must throw their sticks.

The player who gets the most Poohsticks in the pail or tub wins.

> *"I* think we all ought to play Poohsticks."
>
> *The House at Pooh Corner*

This game can be played sitting in a circle, indoors or out—
on the floor, on the grass, or at a table. You will need a bee,
which you can make out of a bean bag or a potato. You will
also need a record player or somebody to play an instrument.

The object of the game is to get rid of the "Bee" as
quickly as possible, and before the music stops. Whoever is
caught with the "Bee" has been "stung" and is "Out." That
player must leave the circle.

Be sure to have a record ready to play on the record
player. If someone is going to play an instrument, explain
the game to him, so he will know that he is to stop playing
every few minutes in the middle of a phrase.

TO MAKE A BEAN-BAG BEE

Draw the outline of a bee 7 to 10 inches long on a piece of
paper.

Cut it out.

Draw the outline of wings. Cut them out.

Take a piece of old sheet, pillow case, or other material.
Fold it in half. Draw around your two patterns on the material.

Cut them out.

Sew the sides together twice with small stitches (the back
stitch is good) , leaving one end open.

Pull the sewn end through the open end.

Paint stripes on its tail and big black eyes on its head.

Stuff it about ⅔ full with dried beans, scraps of cloth, wool, or paper until it is a good bee shape.

Cut the wings out of the same material and color them black, or better still, cut them out of black material. Sew them onto the bee, in back of the eyes.

These make lovely prizes or favors.

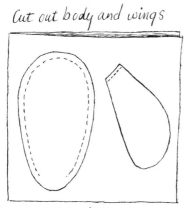

Cut out body and wings

Fold cloth

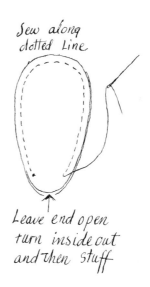

Sew along dotted line

Leave end open turn inside out and then stuff

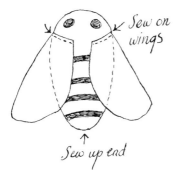

Sew on wings

Sew up end

Bean Bag Bee

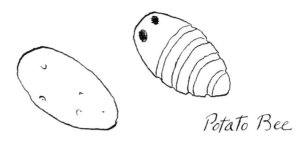

Potato Bee

TO MAKE A POTATO BEE

Choose a medium-size potato, one with rounded ends which is most like the shape of a bee.

Pare stripes around the end you decide to make the tail and cut big eyes at the head end.

Color the stripes orange, and the eyes black, with felt-tipped pens.

"Christopher—*ow!*—Robin," called out the cloud.

"Yes?"

"I have just been thinking, and I have come to a decision. *These are the wrong sort of bees.*"

Winnie-the-Pooh

HONEY POTS

One player is chosen to be Christopher Robin, the store-keeper. A second player is chosen to be Pooh, the customer, who wants to buy some Honey Pots.

The rest of the players squat down and clasp their hands under their knees, pretending to be Honey Pots on a store counter.

Pooh arrives and asks the price of the honey. He walks along one side of the row of Honey Pots while the store-keeper walks along on the other side, telling him the flavors and prices of the different honeys. Pooh pretends to sample the honey in the various pots by touching each player on the head and licking his own paw.

When Pooh chooses one of the Honey Pots and says, "*This* Honey Pot" and touches the player on the head, the player must run and try to reach HOME without being caught by Christopher Robin. HOME can be a tree, a large stone, the corner of a house, garage, or other spot.

If he is caught, then Pooh becomes Christopher Robin, and the player who was caught becomes Pooh.

The game continues until all the players have had a chance to be Christopher Robin or Pooh.

The winner in each game is the player who is not caught.

He could see the honey, he could smell the honey, but he couldn't quite reach the honey.

Winnie-the-Pooh

One player is chosen to be the Pooh-Ghost. He hides in a secret place, such as a Heffalump Trap.

A second player is chosen to be Christopher Robin. The rest of the players are all his friends, the Pooh characters.

Christopher Robin sends Piglet, first, to fetch Pooh's honey pot from the Heffalump Trap. When Piglet does not return, he sends Rabbit. When Rabbit does not return, he sends Owl, then Eeyore, and so on, until the last of his friends does not return.

Then Christopher Robin sets out to find them. When he does, he, too, is captured by the Pooh-Ghost and put in the Heffalump Trap.

The Pooh-Ghost says that he is going to find a Herrible Hoffalump or the Hoffable Hellerump, who is very fierce, to put in the Trap with them. He pretends to lock the Trap and goes off.

As soon as he is out of sight, Christopher Robin and his friends escape and call, "Help! Help! Help!" Whereupon the Pooh-Ghost turns around and chases them.

The Pooh-Ghost puts each player he catches back in the Trap. The first player to be caught becomes Christopher Robin for the next round of the game. The last player to be caught is the winner and the Pooh-Ghost for the next game.

"Help, help!" cried Piglet, "a Heffalump,
a Horrible Heffalump! Help, help, a Herrible
Hoffalump! Hoff, Hoff, a Hellible Horralump!
Holl, Holl, a Hoffable Hellerump!"

Winnie-the-Pooh

V

A WOOZLE-WIZZLE
SNOW PARTY

Piglet said that he had nothing
to do until Friday, and would
be delighted to come.

Winnie-the-Pooh

"It is either Two Woozles and one, as it might be, Wizzle, or Two, as it might be, Wizzles and one, if so it is, Woozle."

Winnie-the-Pooh

Invitations

Use a piece of lightweight red cardboard or heavy red paper, and on it trace a circle around the lid of a pan or the bottom of a can. Be sure the circle is the right size to fit the envelopes the invitations will be mailed in.

Make as many of these as you will need invitations and one or two extra in case you make a mistake or decide to invite a new friend.

Draw or trace any picture you like with Woozle and Wizzle tracks, from Chapter III of *Winnie-the-Pooh*. If you would like to print the tracks on your invitation, mold them from modeling clay or cut them out of a pencil eraser.

To print, press either the modeling clay or eraser tracks onto an inked stamp pad, and press around the picture and the inside edge of your invitation.

If you use red paper for your invitation, black crayon or ink for the Woozle and Wizzle tracks, green stripes for Piglet's scarf and shirt, and white for Pooh's shirt, you will have a good holiday invitation.

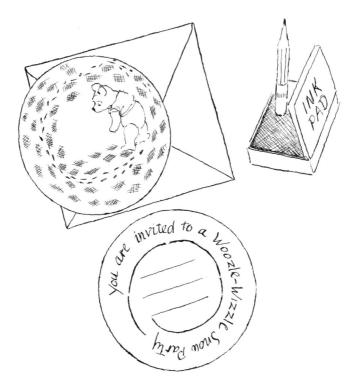

Turn the invitation over and write, also in a circle, starting at the outer edge and working toward the center:

You are invited to a Woozle-Wizzle Snow Party
on *(day)*   , *(date)*   ,
from   o'clock to   o'clock.

Please let me know if you can come.

In the center of the circle write:

(your name)
(address)
(telephone number)

Decorations

TABLECLOTH, TABLE MATS, NAPKINS, PAPER PLATES AND CUPS

Use an old clean sheet—white or with red or green stripes —that has been freshly laundered and pressed, or a white paper tablecloth and napkins.

Decorate them with Woozle and Wizzle tracks from Chapter III of *Winnie-the-Pooh* and from Chapter I of *The House at Pooh Corner,* which you can draw, trace, or print on.

Do the same with paper napkins, which make good table mats when they are flattened or ironed out, and with paper plates and cups.

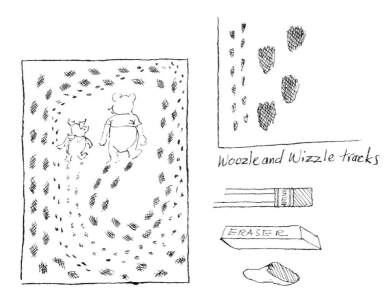

Woozle and Wizzle tracks

CENTERPIECE

A glass bowl full of Honey Popcorn Balls (see page 115) of white, red, and green, or of white only, makes a lovely decoration for the center of your party table, along with Christmas Candles (see page 128).

Or pile them up in the shape of a fir tree in the center of the party table on a piece of foil, a tray, or cake plate.

There should be at least one Honey Popcorn Ball for each friend who comes to your party to hang on his Christmas tree.

"It goes on the table and you put things on it."

The House at Pooh Corner

Things to Eat and Drink

TURKEY OR CHICKEN POT PIE

(Preheat oven to 400° F. for pie crust
450° F. for biscuits)

1 pie crust *or* buttermilk biscuits
3 Tablespoons butter *or* margarine
½ cup diced celery
½ cup thinly sliced onions
3 Tablespoons flour
1½ cups turkey *or* chicken stock *or* canned clear chicken broth
2 cups turkey *or* chicken, cooked and cubed

½ lb. sweet sausage, thinly sliced
1 Tablespoon lemon juice
1 Tablespoon chopped parsley
1 cup fresh *or* frozen peas
pimiento, cut in strips
salt and pepper (to taste)
grated American, Swiss, *or* Parmesan cheese

Put the butter or margarine in a frying pan and sauté the celery and onion in it for 5 minutes.

Add the flour and stir until smooth. Cook 1 minute.

Slowly add the turkey or chicken and the stock in which it has been simmering, the slices of sausage, lemon juice, parsley, peas, and pimiento.

Season with salt and pepper.

Pour into the casserole and cover with the pie crust.

Bake until the crust is almost done, about 35 minutes, and sprinkle with grated cheese.

Return to the oven until the cheese has melted and the top is golden brown.

If you like, after you fill the casserole with the turkey or chicken mixture, cover it with buttermilk biscuits and bake in a very hot oven until the biscuits are done.

This dish may be prepared the day before the party and refrigerated. The pie crust should be baked but not browned, about 20 minutes. To finish cooking, preheat oven to 400° F. and bake for 15 minutes. Sprinkle the pie crust with grated cheese. Bake another 10 to 12 minutes, until the cheese has melted and the top is golden.

"But you said," began Pooh—"you *said* that Tiggers like everything except honey and haycorns."

"*And* thistles," said Tigger, who was now running round in circles with his tongue hanging out.

The House at Pooh Corner

BUTTER BEAR COOKIES

(Preheat oven to 350° F.)

2 cups (4 sticks) butter, softened
1 large egg
1 teaspoon vanilla

1 Tablespoon honey
4–4½ cups sifted, all-purpose flour

Using Pooh and His Friends in this book (pages 138–145), make shapes of heavy cardboard, the same size as you want your cookies.

Whip the softened butter with the egg, vanilla, and honey.

Beat the flour in, 1 cup at a time until 3 cups are mixed, and then add ¼ cup at a time, until the cookie dough is no longer sticky and will hold a shape.

Divide it into four batches.

Roll out one batch ¼ inch thick, and make cookie shapes of Pooh characters by cutting around the cardboard with a sharp knife. Rounded corners are less likely to burn than sharp ones.

Without using cardboard shapes, roll a generous Tablespoon of dough for the second batch of cookies between the palms of your hands, flatten and shape as you would clay into Poohs, Piglets, Owls, etc.

Use the rest of the dough as you like—to make more Pooh or Christmas cookies.

When baking, be sure the cookies on each baking sheet are the same thickness and roughly the same size, so that they take the same baking time, 18 to 20 minutes on an average.

Eat plain or with honey.

JAM TEA FOR SIX

6 Tablespoons seedless jam, any fruit

6 teaspoons honey

4 teaspoons lemon juice

hot water

6 small curls lemon peel

Stir the jam, honey, and lemon juice together in a heated teapot.

Add hot water.

Cover and let steep a minute or two.

Add a curl of lemon peel to each cup.

HOT CRANBERRY JUICE ICE CREAM OR SHERBET CUP

2 quarts cranberry juice or apple cider

1 pint ice cream or sherbet

Heat the cranberry juice or apple cider. Do not boil.

Pour it into a punch bowl.

Add vanilla ice cream, cherry nougat ice cream, or orange sherbet.

Serve as soon as the ice cream or sherbet begins to melt.

Things to Make and Games to Play

HONEY-RAISIN CANDY BASKETS

(Yield: about 24 1″ balls)

confectioners' sugar	½ cup shredded *or* flaked
1½ cups raisins	coconut
½ cup finely chopped nuts	2 Tablespoons honey

Put a layer of confectioners' sugar about ½ inch deep on a
flat plate or pan.

Mix all the other ingredients thoroughly with your hands.

Roll into balls, a heaping teaspoon at a time.

Roll the balls around on the confectioners' sugar on the
plate or pan until powdered.

Let stand 1 or 2 hours to dry.

Wrap in wax paper and Christmas paper to give as presents.

These make lovely baskets to hold candies or nuts. Stand
them on the table on plastic wrap or foil.

To make Honey-Raisin Candy Baskets, take a Tablespoon
or more at a time, make a well in the center and a handle
across the top.

"Did he say Good-bye-and-thank-
you-for-a-nice-time?" said Rabbit.

The House at Pooh Corner

HONEY-ALMOND BRITTLE
FOR PRESENTS

2 Tablespoons butter	¾ Tablespoon salt (if
¼ cup honey	almonds are unsalted)
1 cup almonds *or* other nuts	aluminum foil, 12″ square
1 teaspoon vanilla	*or* larger

Melt the butter in a heavy-bottomed saucepan.

Add the honey and the nuts.

Stir over medium heat until deep brown.

Add the vanilla and salt, if necessary, and stir to mix.

Pour out onto the aluminum foil.

Let it cool before eating or breaking into pieces to put on a candy dish for the party or in a box lined with wax paper as a present.

"It just shows what can be done by taking a little trouble," said Eeyore.

The House at Pooh Corner

HONEY POPCORN BALLS
AND SCULPTURES

1 cup sugar	raisins, nuts, and one *or*
⅓ cup honey	more of the following:
1 cup water, scant	maraschino cherries,
¼ cup (½ stick) butter	date and fig pieces,
1 teaspoon salt	candied friut
4–5 quarts popcorn	10 8″ lengths of ribbon *or*
1 cup cold water	Christmas string
food coloring	

In a heavy-bottomed saucepan stir and bring to a boil the sugar, honey, water, butter, and salt over low heat.

Turn up the heat to medium but *do not stir.*

Boil the syrup about 10 minutes until a drop of it forms a ball in a cup of cold water or to 290° F. on a candy thermometer.

Divide the popcorn into as many bowls as you want colors.

Pour the syrup into another set of bowls and the same number as you want colors.

Stir in the different food colors, a drop at a time.

Coat one bowl of popcorn with one color syrup and shape into Christmas balls, or Pooh shapes—Pooh, Piglet, Owl, Eeyore, and all the rest. Use the raisins, nuts, and fruit to make eyes, mouths, and noses.

If you want to hang the Christmas Popcorn Balls from a tree, put a length of ribbon or string inside the ball as you shape it and tie the ribbon or string in a loop.

Without string, these may be used as decoration, piled high on a flat dish or cake stand in the shape of a fir tree, or any other Christmas shape.

"How do you do Nothing?" asked Pooh, after he had wondered for a long time.

The House at Pooh Corner

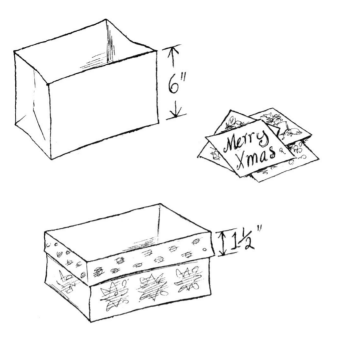

CHRISTMAS TRAYS

1 brown paper bag with a
    square bottom for each
    friend at the party
red, gold, green, *or* silver
    paper *or* last year's Christ-
    mas cards

crayons, colored pens or
    pencils
rubber cement, paste, *or* glue
gold, silver, red, *or* green
    string *or* yarn
blunt-nosed scissors

Make one tray for each friend who will be at your Woozle-
Wizzle Snow Party, or let each friend make his or her own
    at the party.
Measure the open bag 6 inches up from the bottom and
    draw a line across the bag.
Cut off the top of the bag along the line.
Fold down about 1½ inches from the top of the tray to make
    a cuff.

Decorate around the cuff and the outside of the tray with plenty of snowflakes and Woozle-Wizzle tracks.

Cut pieces of Christmas-colored paper or last year's Christmas cards to fit inside the tray.

Paste, glue, or cement them on.

Put in each tray an assortment of colored paper or last year's Christmas cards or other holiday cards; crayons, colored pens or pencils; Christmas-colored string or yarn; a pair of blunt-nosed scissors.

GIFT TAGS

If you have made Christmas Trays for each guest (see page 117), you will have everything necessary for making gift tags.

If you have not, then have plenty of construction paper or holiday and other cards that you have saved up; string or yarn in holiday colors, silver and gold; blunt-nosed scissors.

You will also need a darning needle for each two friends.

Draw gift tags of different sizes and shapes on construction paper—oblongs, squares, circles, triangles. Make some double tags by folding the paper in half before cutting it.

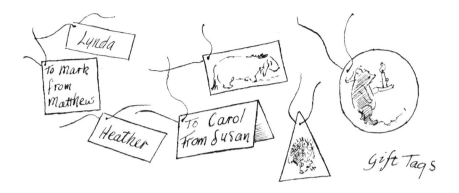

Gift Tags

Draw Pooh designs on the tags from Chapter I of *The House at Pooh Corner,* or Pooh holding a candle (Chapter II of the same book) and cozy scenes, such as the one at the end of Chapter VII in *The House at Pooh Corner* or in Chapter IV of *Winnie-the-Pooh,* and any others you like. Some friends may want to sew little designs like snowflakes or fir trees or cones on the cards in white or green and brown yarn. See Yarn Painting (page 132).

Make the tags big enough to print TO: and FROM: on, then your friends' names, and, if you like, a holiday greeting.

You may also want to cut old holiday or other cards into gift tags by cutting a square, oblong, or other shape around a picture, a part of a picture, or a design. You will often be able to make as many as six tags from one big card.

To tie the tags onto gift packages, thread a darning needle with string or yarn and pull it through one end of the card.

Tie the string or yarn with a knot to the card.

POOH HOLIDAY AND POST CARDS

post-card-weight paper *or*   ruler
   lightweight cardboard   pencil
scissors   crayons *or* paints

HOLIDAY CARDS

Fold paper or cardboard so that you use all of it—usually in half and then in half again.

Cut out the cards—double cards or single.

On the front of each card, draw scenes which are appropriate for the season of the year—Christmas, birthday, Hallowe'en, Easter, and other holidays—from any of the Pooh books.

Paint or color the scenes.

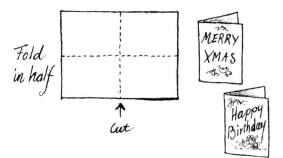

Holiday Cards

Post card

Back   Front

Dear Hardé
Wish you
were here
Love
Claire

ADDRESS

3½"

5½"

POST CARDS

If you want to make post cards, measure off your paper in post-card sizes—at least 5½ inches wide and 3½ inches deep.

Draw and paint Pooh scenes on the front of the cards.

Draw a pencil line down the center or not quite the center on the back of the card. On the right side of the line, draw lines to show where the name and address go and a stamp shape at top right. The left side of the line is for the message.

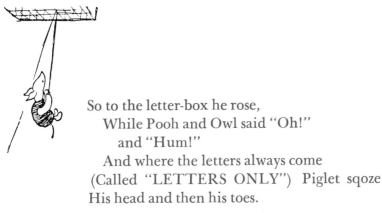

So to the letter-box he rose,
   While Pooh and Owl said "Oh!"
     and "Hum!"
And where the letters always come
(Called "LETTERS ONLY") Piglet sqoze
His head and then his toes.

The House at Pooh Corner

PAPER TREE BELLS

Gold, silver, or colored paper of any kind that has stiffness enough to hold its shape, or even large Christmas cards saved from other years, are fine for making these decorations to hang on a tree, at a window, from a chandelier or light fixture or shade pull.

Use pot lids, pie plates, plastic cups and saucers—anything round that can be drawn around to make a circle—in at least three sizes.

You will need pencil, scissors, straws, beads, and yarn, string, or narrow ribbon.

Draw three or more circles, each one smaller than the last, on paper of the same or different colors.

Cut them out.

Measure across each circle and put a dot in the center.

Cut a pie-shaped piece out of each circle up to the center dot, or cut the circles in half, and glue or paste one edge of the pie shape or half circle over the other, leaving a hole in the center big enough to run a string, yarn, or narrow ribbon through.

Cut up plastic or paper straws in several colors in pieces about 1 inch long. If you have large beads, these are fine, too, and may be used with or instead of the pieces of straw.

Put several knots in the end of the string or ribbon, so that the beads or straw won't fall off.

Put several pieces of straw and beads in different combinations of colors or of the same color on your string, yarn, or ribbon up to about 4 inches.

Thread on the largest bell. If the bell slips down over the plastic straw or bead, remove the bell and tie a knot above the top straw. Thread the bell on again, and continue using straw and bells until you have threaded on the smallest bell.

Add another bead, a straw and a bead, and you have a Tree Bell.

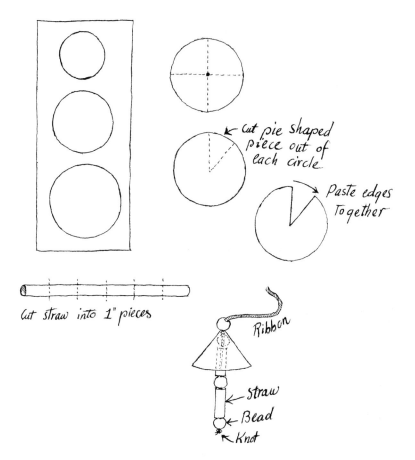

Cut pie shaped piece out of each circle

Paste edges together

Cut straw into 1" pieces

Ribbon

Straw

Bead

Knot

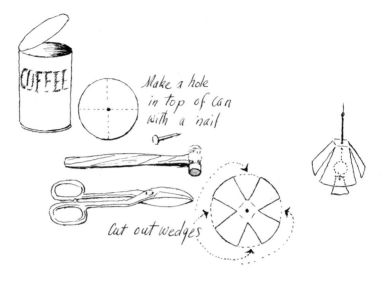

Make a hole
in top of can
with a nail

Cut out wedges

TIN TREE BELLS

tops and bottoms of tin cans,　string
　　all sizes　　　　　　　　　½″ bead
pencil　　　　　　　　　　utility scissors
hammer and nail

Measure to the exact center of the tin-can circle and mark it with a pencil dot.

Pound a hole with the hammer and nail through the dot.

Draw a pencil line from top to bottom and another from side to side to make a cross.

On the rim of the circle measure ½ inch on each side of the pencil lines and mark with a dot. Draw lines toward the center from each dot, stopping ½ inch short of the center hole, making four pie shapes.

Cut out the four pie shapes with a utility scissors.

Use one pie shape as a bell clapper and hammer a hole in the pointed end.

Thread a string through the hole in the clapper, add a bead, and knot it about ¼ to ½ inch above the bead.

Push the string through the center hole in the tin-can circle and double it back, tying a knot just above the center hole to make a loop on top of the bell.

Push down the four sides just below the points of the four pie shapes, and you have a bell that tinkles and can be hung on a tree, in a window, or with greens and ribbons on a door where you will hear the lovely tinkling when the wind blows or you open the door to a friend.

Then Piglet (PIGLET) thought a thing:
   "Courage!" he said. "There's always hope.
   I want a thinnish piece of rope.
Or, if there isn't any bring
A thickish piece of string."

The House at Pooh Corner

STARS

Fold a square of silver, gold, or colored paper so that the four corners meet in the center.

Cut halfway up the center from the middle of the bottom of each triangle made by the fold (cut where the dotted lines are).

Fold each point of the four-pointed star from the cut to the center of the point. Make sure each point is kept sharp.

Fold two of these and paste, cement, or glue them together on the folded sides.

Run a string, ribbon, or length of yarn through one point, so that you can hang the star on a Christmas tree or anywhere else it will add to the holiday decoration.

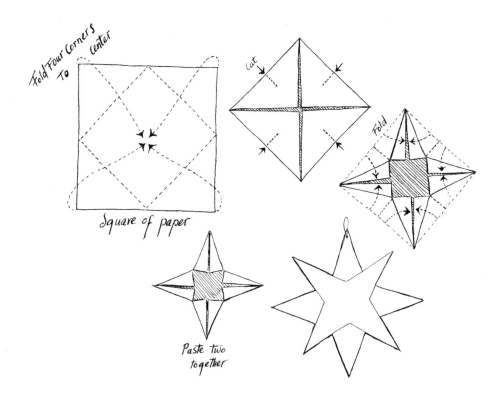

Fold Four Corners To center

Square of paper

Cut

Fold

Paste two together

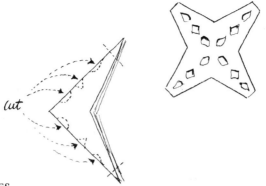

SNOWFLAKES

Fold two stars out of white, silver, or gold paper. Cut off the points.

Fold them in half, and half again. Draw snowflake designs on them.

Cut out the designs.

"And I know it *seems* easy," said Piglet to himself, "but it isn't *every one* who could do it."

The House at Pooh Corner

CHRISTMAS CANDLES

juice *or* condensed-milk cans
paraffin *or* candle ends to melt
old crayons, cut up, one color
    for each candle

enamel pan
mixing spoon
candle ends *or* string
    to use as wicks

Save up as many used juice or condensed-milk cans as you will have friends at your party. Wash and dry them thoroughly after removing the tops.

If you have no candle ends to use as wicks, then dip three strings, which you braid together, in melted paraffin. Be sure to cut the strings about one inch deeper than the can.

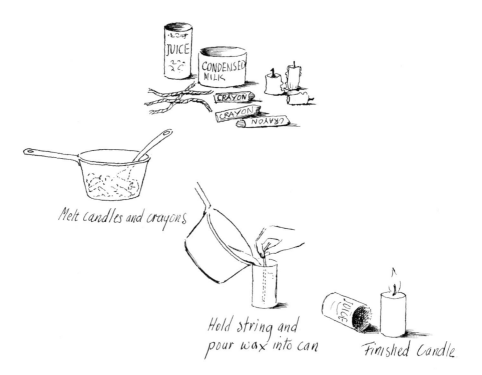

Melt candles and crayons

Hold string and pour wax into can

Finished Candle

Stand the cans on a tray or on paper plates covered with foil or wax paper. Put a candle end or string in each can.

Add the cut-up wax crayon of one color to the paraffin or candle ends in the enamel pan. The wax crayon and paraffin won't stick to the pan if it's enamel. The crayon color should be the same as the color of the candle ends.

Stir and keep over low heat. Mix until the colored crayon is thoroughly blended.

When the paraffin or candle ends have melted and the color has run through the melted wax, put the candle end in the can and the lip of the pan on one side of the juice or milk can. If you use paraffined string, hold it at one end and let it hang in the center of the can.

Pour the paraffin slowly into the can to fill it.

Let it cool and harden. Remove from the can.

If you want to frost your candles, beat a little of the hot paraffin with a fork and apply it with a knife to the sides of the candle.

These can be used as favors for the party table. Be sure you have one candle for each friend.

Pooh was just going to say "Hallo!" for the fourth time when he thought that he wouldn't, so he said: "Who it is?" instead.

"Me," said a voice.

"Oh!" said Pooh. "Well, come here."

So whatever-it-was came here, and in the light of the candle he and Pooh looked at each other.

The House at Pooh Corner

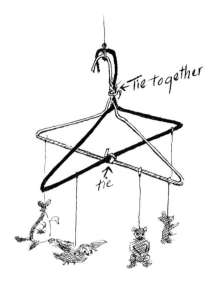

POOH·MOBILE

2 wire coat hangers *or* a plastic bottle carrier from a 6- or 8-pack of canned beverages
heavy thread *or* thin wire
cardboard, foil, *or* plastic

string, ribbon, *or* yarn
paints *or* crayons
scissors
big-eyed needle
nylon *or* linen thread
rubber cement

Use two wire coat hangers, one inside the other to make a cross. Tie them together at the top and bottom with strong thread or thin wire.

Or, use a plastic bottle carrier such as canned sodas or other canned beverages come in. This will bend, but that makes no difference.

Make drawings or tracings of all the Pooh characters or of any one of them alone in many poses on cardboard, foil, or plastic. Color or paint them.

Cut them out.

Thread a big-eyed needle with a sturdy thread or a length of yarn—nylon or linen thread is very good.

Knot the end of the thread or yarn and pull it through the top of one cutout.

Remove the needle.

Use a different length of thread or yarn for each cutout.

Wind the free ends of the thread or yarn onto the wire hangers or the bottle carrier, several times, and then tie.

Balance them. You will have to tie and re-tie some of them to get them to balance and hang properly. Once balanced, dab a little rubber cement on each knot to keep it in place.

Run string, ribbon, or yarn where the hangers are tied together or through the finger holes on the bottle carrier, so that you can hang your mobile.

"For Pooh?" said Eeyore. "Of course it is. The best bear in all the world."

Winnie-the-Pooh

YARN PAINTING
OF TIGGER, POOH, OR OWL

heavy paper *or* lightweight   pencil
   cardboard   rubber cement
yarn, various colors   scissors
pen *or* crayon

Cut a rectangle about 4½ by 5¾ inches from heavyweight paper or lightweight cardboard.

Draw the face of Tigger, Pooh, Owl, or any of the others on it in pencil, full face.

Color the eyes with pen or crayon.

Put a thin coat of rubber cement on the drawing, inside the outline.

For Tigger: Lay strips of yarn—yellow and black to get a Tigger effect—on the cemented drawing. Here and there add a little white yarn, around the eyes, for instance.

Give him a black nose and eyes.

For Pooh: Wind the yarn round and round on the ears and on Pooh's cheeks.

Put a wad of cotton for Pooh's snout. And a black wool nose and eyes.

For Owl: Wind the yarn of one color in a triangle at the top of Owl's head with one long loop for Owl's nose.

Wind the yarn of the second color around the black wool eyes and around the nose.

Now you'll be able to do Piglet, Kanga, Roo, and the others.

Make as many as you like—the same size or larger—and trim off the excess paper around your Yarn Painting, if you like.

"I am calling it this," said Owl importantly, and he showed them what he had been making.

The House at Pooh Corner

CATCH THE WOOZLE

This is an outdoor game to play in the snow.

Tramp out a big circle in the snow with Woozle, Wizzle, or boot tracks.

Choose one player to be Pooh or "It."

Pooh calls to one player to be the Woozle. He must run clockwise around the circle in front of the other players, who stand at regular distances from each other on the tramped-out circle.

Pooh tries to catch him before he dodges in behind a standing player. If Pooh doesn't catch him, then the player the Woozle dodged behind becomes the Woozle and must run.

This continues until Pooh catches a running Woozle, then the Woozle becomes Pooh or "It" and must try to catch another player.

"Tracks," said Piglet. "Paw-marks."
He gave a little squeak of excitement.
"Oh, Pooh! Do you think it's a–a–a Woozle?"

Winnie-the-Pooh

POOH CLUES

Choose twelve short quotations from *Winnie-the-Pooh* that have drawings which illustrate them.

Make twelve cards the size of playing cards with the quotations and twelve with the matching drawings. Number both with the same number from 1 to 12.

Make a twenty-fifth card on which you draw a picture of Pooh licking a honey pot with a quotation about honey.

This is a game for three, four, or five players. The object is to get as many pairs of matching picture and quotation cards as you can *and* the twenty-fifth card with the picture and quotation of Pooh and the honey pot.

Deal the cards. The dealer is the first "asker," and he asks each player in turn for a card he needs to match one in his hand. He begins by asking the player on his left and goes around the circle. His turn ends when a player does not have the card asked for. The player on the dealer's left is the next asker and begins by asking the player on *his* left.

Whenever the asker thinks he knows which player has the twenty-fifth card, he may ask for it. If he is wrong, then he loses his turn the next time around. Remember that if you ask for the twenty-fifth card and get it, all the other players will know you have it and will ask for it. The object will be to ask for the twenty-fifth Pooh card when you have all matching pairs and need only the twenty-fifth card to go out. With all matching pairs and the Pooh card, you score 25 points.

A player may go out without holding the twenty-fifth card if he holds all matching pairs, but his score is only 10 points.

With three players, each asker may ask only the player to his left for a card he needs when it is his turn.

Later on, when they had all said
"Good-bye" and "Thank-you" to
Christopher Robin, Pooh and Piglet
walked home thoughtfully together
in the golden evening, and for a
long time they were silent.

Winnie-the-Pooh

POOH AND HIS FRIENDS
FOR TRACING

Christopher Robin

138 *Pooh and His Friends for Tracing*

Pooh

WOL

Piglet

Pooh and His Friends for Tracing 141

Rabbit

Pooh and His Friends for Tracing

A. A. MILNE was born in England in 1882, studied at Westminster School and Cambridge University, and for several years was an editor of *Punch*. In 1924 he wrote *When We Were Very Young,* a book of verse dedicated to his only son, Christopher Robin Milne. In 1926 *Winnie-the-Pooh,* which contains the first ten Pooh stories, was published, followed in 1927 by another book of verse, *Now We Are Six.* In 1928 more Pooh stories appeared in *The House at Pooh Corner.* Milne died in 1956.

VIRGINIA H. ELLISON grew up near Poughkeepsie, New York, and was graduated from Vassar College. She lives in Stamford, Connecticut, and has two grown sons. Mrs. Ellison has been an editor and writer for a number of years. Her first Pooh-inspired book, *The Pooh Cook Book,* a collection of original recipes for all occasions, was published in 1969.

ERNEST H. SHEPARD was born in 1879 and lives in Sussex, England. He illustrated all four of the Pooh books, and it is difficult to think of Pooh and his friends apart from Shepard's marvelous drawings. He also illustrated another children's classic, *The Wind in the Willows,* by Kenneth Grahame, as well as several stories of his own.

GRAMBS MILLER, who was born in Peking, China, of American parents, did the charming pen-and-ink explanatory drawings. She came to the United States to study art when she was seventeen, and now illustrates books for both adults and children. Miss Miller and her writer-husband live in New York City.